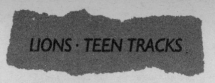

LIONS · TEEN TRACKS

It's My Life

"You're playing hard to get," Sharon had said as Jan walked off, away from school and from Peter Carey's invitation to the college disco on Friday night. Was she? Jan didn't really know. She wanted time to think things out, ask Mum what she thought.

But when Mum doesn't come home, Jan finds her own problems taking second place, as she is expected to cope with running the house for her father and younger brother Kevin, as well as studying for exams and trying to sort out her feelings towards Peter. Slowly she realises what sort of life her mother led, the loneliness and the pressures she faced, and with this realisation comes Jan's firm resolve that despite the expectations of family, neighbours and friends, she will decide things for herself; after all, "It's my life".

Robert Leeson

It's My Life

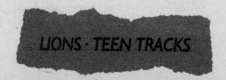

LIONS · TEEN TRACKS

First published 1980 by William Collins Sons & Co. Ltd
First published in Lions Teen Tracks 1981
Ninth impression November 1988

Lions Teen Tracks is an imprint of
the Children's Division, part of
the Collins Publishing Group,
8 Grafton Street, London W1X 3LA

for Christine

Chapter 1

Peter Carey cut across the scrum by the gate as the school-yard emptied and stopped in front of Jan.

"Doing anything on Friday night?"

For a second she was stuck for words, embarrassed. She made a face and shrugged. He went on.

"There's a disco at the college . . ."

Their eyes crossed. The wind whipped the scarf across his face and Jan thought of Dick Turpin. He wasn't asking her. He was telling her.

"I'll let you know."

As she spoke Jan heard her friend Sharon gasp. You didn't do that to Pete. But the words had been spoken before Jan could think of any others. Then she clenched her teeth to stop any other words coming out.

In a fraction of a second she could sense Pete's surprise and annoyance. But he kept a straight face She could see that much-admired brain of his ticking over.

Then he said, "Right!" turned away and was gone.

Now there were just a handful of girls by the gate around Jan and Sharon. Jan wanted to move away quickly, but Sharon held her back.

"How do you manage it?"

"Manage what?" asked Jan, edging away.

"Oh, come on Jan. You know what I mean."

"Don't." Jan was half-mocking her friend but to her surprise Sharon looked upset.

"I'd have said 'yes' right off."

"Well, Sharon love, you're not me and that's a good job."

"What d'you mean?"

Jan stared at Sharon, baffled by the change in Sharon's voice. She tried to laugh it off.

"Well, if you were me, I couldn't put up with you, could I?"

"Stop mickey-taking," said Sharon. "Why didn't you tell him straight out 'yes' or 'no'?"

What was Sharon so narky about all of a sudden? Jan wondered. She began to reach out to touch her friend's arm, when Tina Ellis, loudest mouth in the small group still hanging round the school gates, spoke up – half to her friends, half to the world:

"Some people don't know what it's for."

Jan swung round.

"Some people don't even know where it is," she retorted.

Tina stopped, mouth open. Her friends sniggered. Sharon's expression grew more sullen. Jan wondered why she had to be so quick with her answers. She didn't mean it, but Sharon didn't always understand that.

The backchat had got her clear of the crowd. But Sharon stayed inside the gate as if she were willing Jan not to go. Jan shifted her bag from hand to hand. She shrugged and the shrug turned to a shiver.

"I'm freezing."

She took a step along the pavement. The other girls drifted away. Sharon still did not move.

"See you tomorrow, Sha-"

"I know what it is, Jan. You're playing hard to get."

"Oh, shut your face."

"Charming."

That had done it. Sharon had something real to be narky about, now. But Jan was away, striding down Gorse Lane, nose pointed towards home.

"Bye," she called, without turning.

There was no answer. Ah well, couldn't be helped. She'd be extra nice to Sharon tomorrow. But right now she wanted to walk and think, not talk.

Jan's foot landed in a puddle and splashed her tights. She had been clumping down Gorse Lane like a hiker, looking neither to left nor right.

She looked around. There was the junior school, and a handful of kids still loitered in the road, dodging the cars. Her brother Kev wasn't among them. He must be home by now.

She heard voices. Women were coming out of the works' gate at Cartwright Electronics. Mum had taken her in there some time back – a great, glaring, steel and glass cave, with six hundred women all putting screws in switches, screws in plugs, picking up, putting down, chatting, giggling, singing, making faces behind the back of the pink-faced supervisor as he paced to and fro. Mum had got out of production six months ago and was working in Personnel: phone answering, typing, coming home later and later – always a rush on, always a crisis.

Jan stopped. Should she hang on? Maybe Mum would be coming out now and they could walk home arm in arm and chat a bit before they got home and Kev started hanging around, yakking and nagging. The wall of the old people's home loomed on her right, tall, blackened and bulging. Years ago, when she was in the juniors, she and Mum would play a game, holding hands and running quickly past the wall before it came tumbling down. Jan found herself walking faster, almost running, then caught her breath and slowed down. She had nearly run past the turn off for the street where they lived now. It was close to the embankment, two rows of tall, narrow, dark houses. Jan didn't like it.

She paused by their house, feeling in her bag for the key. The neighbour's front door was ajar and the television light flickered in the kitchen down the passage. She heard Kev's shrill laughter. That meant Mum couldn't be home yet, or she'd have had him out of there like a shot.

Jan walked into the tiny front room. From the window you could just see the turning into Gorse Lane. No sign of Mum. The imitation marble clock on the mantelshelf struck the half-hour. Mum must be working late again. Reaching her wasn't easy these days. Mornings were all go, making breakfast, getting Dad off, getting Kev off. Jan fended for herself.

In the evenings, Dad and Mum always seemed to be arguing quietly in corners over money, and Jan would climb to her room and get her books out.

She wandered into the kitchen and put the kettle on. If Mum came now, they could have a chat over a cup of tea. Restlessly she moved back into the front room. Taking a banana from the bowl on the sideboard, she peeled it, and slowly stuffed it into her mouth as she picked up her bag and slouched upstairs. In her mind she could hear Sharon's voice: "It's not fair, you can eat anything; you never put on weight."

In her room she began to peel off her clothes. The reflection in the dressing-table mirror caught her eye. Sharon was right. Nothing, but nothing, made her put on weight. She looked ironically at herself in the mirror. Mum was full-bodied and handsome with a snub nose and auburn hair. Dad was tall, thin and blond with a striking, hooked nose. Jan had got bits from both of them – the wrong bits, Dad's thinness and his big nose, Mum's big breasts (that was embarrassing) and her hair, but not quite, more carrot than auburn.

She stared at the mirror.

"Ginger-headed whippet." That's what the lad on the next landing had called her years ago when they lived on the estate. She'd stuck her finger in his eye. That shut him up – and brought his parents running. There was quite a row. Dad was upset, but Mum took it calmly.

Goose pimples prickled on Jan's skin. She quickly pulled on jumper and jeans and went downstairs. The house was still empty. Steam billowed from the kitchen. She rushed in and switched off the kettle. Brewing the tea – Mum must be home any time now – she opened the fridge and looked for a cold sausage. The shelves were full, meat, cheese, milk, more than usual for this time in the week. Mum had been stocking up. Strange, she was so careful with her spending money, always totting up, doing sums.

The front door went back against the passage wall with a crack.

"Where's Mum?"

Kev charged into the kitchen, then stopped, wrinkling his nose. His plump face was sticky brown with chocolate.

"Oh, it's you," he said.

"Hard luck."

"Where's Mum?"

"Not in my pocket."

"What's for tea?"

"You don't need tea. You've been stuffing yourself, next door. What happened, did they run out of biscuits?"

Kev stuck out his tongue and ran into the front room. Jan sat down on a kitchen stool and poured herself a cup of tea. If Mum didn't come soon, this would be stewed. The clock over the cooker showed half past five. Dad would be home before long. No chance for a word alone with Mum. If she came soon though, Jan could help getting the tea ready, shutting the kitchen door to keep Fatso out.

What could she say? She wanted to talk about Pete and to hear what Mum said. Mum always gave her opinion. Often that was annoying, but sometimes it was like listening to her own thoughts. That was it – she'd talk about it lightly while they laid the table. Only first of all, she'd ask how things had gone at work today. That would get Mum in a good mood, and then they could gossip a bit, have a laugh, chat about it, carelessly.

"You know what, Mum, there's this lad at school, in the sixth . . . I've mentioned him to you . . ."

"First sign of madness, talking to yourself." Kev stood in the kitchen doorway, staring at her.

She started at him.

"Shut up or I'll shut you up."

He backed off, eyes wide.

"What's up with you?" His voice was small, half-scared.

"Why don't you go and watch the box?"

"Nah, there's only the news."

"The what? What time is it?"

Jan looked at the clock again.

"Where's Mum?" whined Kevin.

"I don't know."

"What's for tea?"

"Oh, I don't know. Get yourself some beans."

"Mum says I shouldn't try to open tins."

Controlling her exasperation, Jan went to the cupboard, emptied beans into a pan and put them on to warm. Where was Mum? Had she and Dad arranged to meet somewhere? But no one had said a thing.

"Just keep your eyes on those, give 'em a stir," she told Kevin and went out into the passage. Picking up the phone she dialled Mum's work number. The phone rang and rang at the other end. But, just as she was about to put the phone down again, a man's voice answered:

"Cartwright Electronics."

"Personnel Department, please."

"This is Personnel. Our switchboard closes at five."

"Can I speak to Mrs Whitfield?"

"Mrs Whitfield?" The man's voice, he was young, sounded uncertain.

"Yes, Mrs Whitfield. She works there. This is her daughter."

"Oh." He hesitated, then, "I'm afraid I can't say. She hasn't been in here today."

Chapter 2

Jan stood in the dark passage, phone in hand. The man at the other end had hung up. She frowned. What was Mum up to?

From the kitchen came the smell of burning. She slammed down the phone and rushed in to find Kevin curled up in a chair by the door, while blue smoke rose from the cooker.

"Can you not smell, or something?"

"Mum says I haven't got to touch the cooker."

"She didn't mean it that way and you know it. Anyway, it's your tea." She tipped the blackened mess on to a plate. "Here."

He snorted: "Get off, I'm not having that. Eat it yourself."

She started towards him. He shifted round the table and grumbled:

"Hey, when's Mum coming home?"

"I don't know."

"No need to shout." He dodged out of the kitchen and a moment later she heard the TV go on. She picked up the teapot. It was cold. Taking the plate of beans she emptied it into the pedal bin, piled cups and plates into the sink and marched out, stamping up the stairs. Why didn't Mum let her know she was off somewhere? Why should she have to be lumbered with that pain of a brother?

In her room she emptied her bag, picked out her geography and carried it over to her favourite place – a cane seat by the window. The book fell open where she had left a marker last night, but she could not pick up the thread, staring at the page without seeing the words. Her mind wandered to Pete. Why had he asked her? Sharon was better looking. And, why had she put him off?

Was she playing hard to get? She remembered Sharon's words in the schoolyard. For a flash of a second she was indignant, then grinned to herself, stretched out her legs and inflated her chest. Jan's awful hard to get – but what for?

What was Pete after? He was in the sixth, taking 'A' levels this year, while she was taking her 'O's. He was nearly two years older. But, why hadn't she said yes? Was she playing for time, trying to make her mind up? The funny thing was, she'd got away with it. Maybe that was what made Sharon angry.

The noise of the television boomed up suddenly from the front room then stopped altogether as the street door opened. Jan leapt to the bedroom door then paused.

"Where's your mother, Kevin?"

Father and son stood in the passage below the stairs. Dad was loaded with papers as usual and his face in the hall light was strained.

16

"Dad, I haven't had any tea and our Jan tried to make me eat burnt beans."

"You little creep," Jan shouted down the stairs. Her father stared in amazement at her tousled hair and angry face.

"Is your Mum not home, Jan?"

"No – I," she began. Dad frowned and waved at Kevin.

"You get up to your bedroom and take those outdoor things off."

Kevin vanished and Dad went slowly into the kitchen with Jan following. He stared at the dirty dishes in the sink.

"I thought tea would have been ready by now," he muttered.

"I'll make you a cup."

"No, I need something to eat. I missed my lunch break today."

"Shall I fry you some bacon and egg?"

He made a face. "Hasn't she left anything to warm up?"

She swung the fridge door open. "It's full, Dad. Mum's been out shopping but she hasn't left any meal. I thought you and she were out somewhere."

"Never. She must be working over again. She lives at that flaming firm."

Jan's eyes widened. "No, Dad. She hasn't been in there today. I thought she had . . ."

"How d'you know?"

"I rang."

"You did what?"

17

She hesitated. "I rang work. I wanted to find out . . ." her voice trailed away.

"I wish you hadn't."

"Why, Dad?"

"Well, it's none of their business," he spoke loudly.

"I don't understand."

"Oh, never mind. Put the kettle on, Jan. I'll cut myself some bread."

They moved about the tiny kitchen, dodging each other. Minutes later, when they were both sitting down again, Jan spoke quietly.

"Dad, it's a bit funny, isn't it?"

"What is?"

"I mean, Mum not being here, getting on for seven and not telling you. And not going into work."

He looked uneasily at her. "I don't know, she might have an appointment, dentist or something."

"Oh, no, Dad, she'd have left a note. She always does for things like that. Dad, you don't suppose anything's gone wrong, do you?"

"Eh, what? No, give over, love. What could be wrong?"

The last word came out more strongly. Jan was silent for a moment while her father ate, then:

"Dad, I suppose she couldn't have gone to Gran's?"

He shook his head.

"No, I'd know if she was going over to Warby."

"I didn't mean Warby Gran's. I meant Granny Machen."

"She's not been near them in years. Why should she suddenly go over there now?"

"Someone might be ill."

"I shouldn't think they'd tell her."

Jan sipped her tea. "That's weird, Dad. They are her parents, after all."

He raised his face from his eating and said strangely:

"You know what your Mum once said: 'I'm a voluntary orphan.'"

"That's something I can't imagine," said Jan. "Cutting yourself off from your parents."

He shook his head. "They never wanted her. That's something you don't know about, Jan. We're a close family. We stick together." His voice sounded heavy and deliberate. "That's why I was a bit – peeved – when you rang the works about Mum. I mean, we don't broadcast our family business. We look after things ourselves. The less people know, the better." He got to his feet.

"Look, Jan, can you clear these things away? I want to have a look at these papers." He walked out of the kitchen and she turned to the sink. She was halfway through the washing up when the phone rang. She dropped a cup, chipping a handle, and sprang to the passage. But Dad was there first.

Wrong number.

Jan finished in the kitchen and slowly climbed the stairs again. Her room was grey with dusk, the few pieces of furniture just visible. Her books shone pale on the bedcover. She switched on the light and the darkness sprang up outside, closing in on the windows. She concentrated, read several passages and made notes, then stopped again. She heard voices. Dad was on the landing, talking through the door to Kev.

"Get those things away and get washed now, lad."

Jan looked at her watch. It was coming up to eight

o'clock. She heard Kevin grumbling:

"I'm hungry, Dad. I didn't have a proper tea and our Jan . . ."

"That'll do. Get undressed and washed. I'll bring you up a sandwich."

"All right. Dad, when's Mum coming home?"

"Later."

"When's that?"

"When you're asleep."

"Will she come in and see me?"

"Oh, for – yes, Kev, just get yourself ready for bed."

Jan followed her father downstairs and into the kitchen.

"I thought you didn't know where Mum was."

He glared: "I don't."

"But what did you tell our Kev she'd be home later, for?"

"What else could I tell him? He'd only start mithering otherwise."

"But where can she be?" Jan insisted.

He paused, bread knife in hand. For a moment she thought he was going to shout at her, then he lowered the knife and said quietly:

"I don't know, Jan, I don't know."

The three words chilled her.

"Dad, suppose something *is* wrong. Suppose she's been knocked over."

He swallowed. "Give over, Jan. We'd have heard by now. Bad news travels fast. She must have gone off somewhere on a shopping trip and been held up."

"But, she'd have phoned."

"Well perhaps she couldn't. You know half the phone

boxes are smashed up these days. Perhaps she didn't have any spare coins."

"That doesn't sound like Mum."

"Oh, don't go on, Jan." Suddenly he was irritable again. He picked up the sandwich he'd been making for Kev and strode out of the kitchen. Jan began to put the kettle on again, then stopped. The thought of another cup of tea soured her stomach. Upstairs she heard shouts and bumps. Dad and Kev were playing a chasing game, like two boys. After a while there was silence. She heard doors go, but Dad did not come down.

Several minutes passed in silence. Jan went upstairs again. On the landing, she paused. The door to her parents' bedroom was open. She could see the bed and beyond that the small, cluttered desk under the window, where her father studied at nights.

"Dad." She spoke through the space at the door jamb.

"Yes, Jan?"

"Maybe old Mrs Elsom next door knows something."

"She'd have let us know by now."

"Or whatsername on the other side."

"Catch Mum letting her know anything. Not much."

"Shouldn't we ask?"

She went back to her own room and sat down again. But she did not pick up her books. Instead she stared out of the window as the moments passed. In the quiet back street she heard from a distance a church clock chime. She counted nine.

A strange noise from the next door room caught her ear. She heard the squeak of the wardrobe door and the rustle of clothing as though someone were packing a case. She started up and went to the open door of their bedroom. Dad was busy taking Mum's clothes out of the wardrobe, one by one, coats, dresses, blouses, cardigans, one by one and laying them on the bed, first slowly and then in haste, piling them up.

Suddenly he turned and saw her eyes on him. For a moment, they looked at one another in silence, then he said:

"Jan, I'm going to the police."

Chapter 3

"The police?" Jan felt cold in the pit of her stomach.

Her father began clumsily to put the clothes back on the rail, pushing and stuffing them in. She took them from him and one by one, shook them out, smoothed them down and slid the hangers along the rail. There weren't many dresses, but they seemed to fill the tiny space. As she leaned into the wardrobe to arrange the clothes, Mum's familiar scent rose from them. As it did, the chill from her stomach seemed to rise into her chest.

"They're all there, Jan. She's got nothing with her but her workday outfit. She must have set off to work as usual."

There was a softer, more anxious note in his voice as though irritation had given way to concern. Jan looked at Dad's face shadowed by the weak bedroom light. The features were calm, just that familiar furrow between the eyes, always there when he pored over his reading. But she sensed he was holding himself in.

"I won't be long," he said, turning to pick up his

overcoat which he had thrown over the chair. He moved to pass her but she stopped him.

"Dad, I'm coming with you."

He shook his head. "No, somebody's got to look after Kev."

"Oh, he sleeps like a log. You could drive a truck through his bedroom and he wouldn't wake."

While he hesitated, Jan dodged into her own room and came out pulling on her jacket.

"Jan, suppose Mum gets back, while we're away."

"We'll leave a note, Dad, say we're just down the road. Oh, come on." She was surprised at the edge in her voice. Or was it surprise at the way Dad was behaving – uncertain, almost bewildered.

He pulled his coat round him and joined her on the stairs. His lips moved slightly as if he were speaking to himself and he seemed to be moving himself by an effort. Jan ran on ahead.

"Don't make so much noise, Jan."

But she did not hear him. Outside, the car, an ancient, grey Minor, was parked only feet from the front door which opened directly on to the pavement. In the lamp light, L stickers showed on the nearest wing. Mum had been taking lessons. Her father looked up and down the road and quietly opened the near door to let Jan in.

"They'll think I'm taking you out for lessons now," he murmured as he started the car.

"What does it matter what they think?" Jan started to ask, but she swallowed the words. The car started, jerked, stalled, started and finally moved forward. Dad's hands gripped the wheel hard. He was a careful driver, but tonight he pushed the old car hard, and took the corners sharply, throwing her against the door.

She gasped and stared at him.

"Sorry." He slowed down. They drove on, saying no more until they came to the police station in the high street. Again Dad looked about him as they got out and then he led the way up the stone steps into the building which smelled of age and disinfectant.

Behind the desk sat a fat, white-haired sergeant, collar undone. Behind him, tea mugs in hand, lounged several men, some in uniform, some in plain clothes. Their conversation stopped for a brief, cool inspection of Jan and her father and then went on as if they were not there.

At first Dad spoke so low that the sergeant urged him to speak up. The others stopped talking again and stared. A young constable now eyed Jan over his tea mug, with friendly insolence. She stared back at him for a moment, then deliberately looked away. After a while they began to chat again, and Jan pressed closer along the counter to hear what Dad was saying.

The sergeant looked up from the pad, scratching his nose with the end of his pen.

"How old is your wife, Mr Whitfield?"

"Eh?"

"Your wife, sir, how old?"

Jan felt her father bristle. "What has that got to do with her being missing from home?"

The sergeant shifted his massive shoulders in the blue uniform cloth and his face, a purpling pyramid of flesh resting on great double chins above his open collar, creased in resignation.

"The situation is, sir: if she is under seventeen, we can

make inquiries, sir. If not, we can take no action."

"What? Why?"

The sergeant breathed slowly and noisily.

"Most people, sir, when they go missing, don't want to come back. We can't make them. If they want to come back, well, they just turn up."

"You mean, you won't do anything?"

"Sir, this last year, there were over six thousand people reported missing – and those are just the ones reported to us. We don't have the men to go chasing them."

"You seem to have enough spare hands here tonight."

Jan glanced nervously at her father. There was a new anger, even arrogance in his voice. But the sergeant did not seem to notice.

"Ah, that's now. Later on, when you're in bed like most decent people, we shall be very busy. The people we have to deal with mainly keep different hours to yours – except of course people like demonstrators and pickets – they do their work in broad daylight."

"You're quick enough then . . ." Dad was sharp and the sergeant became official again.

"Mr – Whitfield. Have you any reason to suppose she's in any danger?"

"I don't know. If I did, I wouldn't be wasting my time here."

The bushy white eyebrows went up a fraction.

"I mean, sir, is she a sick person, liable to fainting fits, epileptic, diabetic, such like? Or does she wander off?"

"No, she does not."

"You see, sir, if that were the case . . ." The pale eyes wandered over Jan's father, taking in face, and clothes, then turned slightly to her, weighing them both up.

"Are you on the phone, sir?" He scribbled on the paper.

"We'll keep our eye on the hospitals." He glanced at his pad.

"If anything turns up, we'll let you know, of course. But I shouldn't worry too much. It's probably something quite simple, but, say unforeseen. Just go back home. She's quite likely there already. She's probably . . ."

The purple cheeks creased again as though the sergeant were about to make a joke, but his eye caught Dad's and the witticism was filed away. The sergeant shifted his pad over to one side and put down his pen.

"Good night, sir."

Outside in the car, Dad started the engine and pulled away from the kerb again. He spoke to himself.

"Bloody fool, wasting my time . . ."

"Dad, we had to do it." Jan breathed in deeply to shift the weight inside her. She put her hand on his arm.

"Let's get back home, quickly. If she's back, she'll be worried. I don't know how we'll explain it to her. It'll sound daft, won't it, if she comes home and finds out we've been down to the police station about her?"

As the car pulled up outside their house, she was nearest to the front door, but Dad reached it first. The door banged against the passage wall and the sound echoed. Mum was not there, Jan could tell.

She did not come home that night, nor the next night, nor the next. . . .

Chapter 4

Jan awoke next day to a misery she could not name. As she struggled to get up, downstairs the dead, empty house reminded her again what had happened.

A note on the kitchen table said:

"Taken Kev to school. I've told him Mum's away for a little while. Can you be here when he gets home tonight, and pick up some bread?"

Mum's "away". Well, that was true. She wasn't here. And Jan had to push her body into her clothes, stuff her books into her bag and drag herself off along Gorse Lane to school. She was late. Dad had forgotten to wake her or had let her sleep in. She didn't know which and didn't care.

At the end of that first day, she could remember little of what had happened. Only in the evening, she recalled small incidents like freeze frames in a TV series. Sharon meeting her face to face in the classroom doorway, staring and passing on. But who was not speaking to whom? Another girl, less close, but friendly, coming to her, bright and inquisitive, and Jan putting her off with tight, dull answers. She guessed her class mate was asking her about Pete, but she was thinking about Mum. And once, she remembered, she told another girl to shut up and leave her alone. Her expression, wide, hurt eyes, suddenly came back to Jan at the end of the day. Hurt and be hurt.

She saw Pete from a distance, standing with his mates, outside the sixth form block. She thought he turned towards her, but she walked away across the concourse, hiding behind a crowd of fifth years.

The next day, as she bent over her desk, she saw the face of Miss Maudesley, her tutor, eyes anxious behind large glasses, close to her own, asking some question she could not quite catch. But she answered.

"I'm quite all right, thank you."

She must have spoken loudly for several of her class mates turned and stared. Miss Maudesley walked away, as though offended. Jan knew that she ought to say something, to put things right. But the heaviness in her held her back. Only by the greatest strength of will did she go from day to day, and each word she must speak to others was a burden.

She had gone into a tunnel with no end in sight and no view to left or right – school, home, shops, kitchen, stairs, bedroom, books, work, sleep. She moved so from day to day, from place to place, and did not know how she had reached each point in her familiar round. She saw people, but did not look at them, spoke to them, but did not hear what they said. Nothing was real and nothing could be felt, but the heavy ache deep inside her.

On the fourth day, she found herself in the early evening with women from the works, picking up bits and pieces in the supermarket. The cash lady was thin and sharp-nosed with china-blue eyes and a Mrs Thatcher hairdo. Every six months the supermarket changed hands and she swapped overalls, bright green, dark blue, candy stripe. But she was always there, dipping her head like a sparrow, exchanging genteel backchat with the plump manager, quizzing the customers. She knew everyone, knew all that was going on.

"Not seen your mother lately, love. Is she poorly?"

Jan looked and did not see her, picked up her bag and walked out.

Each night as she came home, Jan would fetch Kevin from next door, looking past the woman there with her broad, handsome face, hard hairdo and low neckline, into the cluttered kitchen with its glaring TV, its haze of cigarette smoke, to call Kev from where he sat between her boys, pushing chocolate into his mouth.

"Mother poorly, love?"

"Away."

"Any time you'd like me to pick up some shopping for you . . ."

"It's all right, thank you very much. We can manage. Kev, are you coming?"

She did not know why she dragged her brother away. She did not even know why she rushed home, just to get his tea. But rush home she did, and dragged Kev away, for all his sullen looks and sometimes open grumbling. And she made him get undressed and into bed in good time, every night. Mum was "away" for a while and everything was going on as though she were still here.

She would make cups of tea for Dad as he sat over his books. He did not drink them. But neither did he look at his books. He stared out of the window. And she returned to her room and opened her books and stared out at the darkening street below.

On Saturday as she stepped out of the front door, someone called her. It was little old Mr Elsom from next door on the other side. A retired railwayman, he still wore a shabby, black waistcoat and collarless, flannel shirt. His crab-apple face was seamed and weathered, and when he stood close you could smell old man's sweat in his clothes.

He took her sleeve.

"Not seen your mother lately, love. I usually give her some potatoes at this time of year. We've got plenty, Edie and I. Always help people, I say, never know when you may need it yourself."

Help? What for? Jan thought she saw an inquisitive gleam in his eye.

"No, thanks, we can manage."

(The picture of his offended face went into the collection in Jan's head: Sharon, Miss Maudesley, other class mates, the supermarket lady, the woman next door – hurt expressions, raised eyebrows, half-open mouths. Sometimes, when she slept, these faces came and crowded round her, saying nothing, only staring, until she woke up in desperation.)

As the days passed she was aware that the burden of running the house had slipped on to her, that Dad was doing nothing but going to his course, coming home, eating a little, letting cups of tea go cold. He was doing nothing, allowing the days to pass, growing more silent, jumping when the phone rang. And it came into her mind that she should complain, speak to him, ask him what he was going to do. But she could not bring herself to throw off this heaviness, to lay herself open to things that might be worse.

One day, at breaktime, she leaned on the wall in the schoolyard. The faint warmth of the April sunshine comforted her somehow. Someone was talking to her. She stared. Tina Ellis was there, bending close and speaking quietly:

"You all right, Jan?"

"Eh?" Tina Ellis and she had never spoken to one another. They'd shouted at each other, and once in the third year, they'd had a fight in the formroom, spilling stuff from desks while others cheered them on.

"Are you all right?"

"Course I am, what d'you mean?"

Tina Ellis was silent, as though weighing up Jan's mood. Then she said:

"Our Mum cleared off – six months back."

Jan pushed up from the wall.

"What are you talking about?" Her voice was hard. Tina's eyes widened.

"Nothing. Forget I said ought. Snob."

She walked away, leaving Jan staring.

But as she walked home that afternoon, she was suddenly aware of a new feeling, an angry resentment, pushing the heavy weariness aside for a moment before it passed. Later in the evening, after she had left a cup of tea on the desk at her father's elbow she went loudly downstairs. In the front room, Kevin sat in front of the television set. She turned it off.

"What was that for?"

"I want some quiet. I'm going to phone." She closed

the front room door firmly behind her. From the book in the drawer beneath the phone, she chose a number, long distance, and dialled.

Her father appeared at the head of the stairs.

"Who are you ringing, Jan?"

"I'm phoning Gran."

"No, you're not."

"Not Warby Gran, the other."

"I've told you, that's no . . ."

But the number was ringing out. Dad started down the stairs, but stopped as Jan began to speak.

"Is that Gran . . . Mrs Machen? This is Jan. It's our Mum. I mean, is she up there with you?"

"No. She hasn't been here since the Christmas before last," came the curt answer.

"It's just that we're worried. She's been away now since the beginning of last week and she's left no word."

"Well, I can't say I'm surprised. She always pleased herself. Never told us anything. She left home twice when she was your age. We had to have the police bring her back. Third time, we told her she could stay away. But she never gave a toss what we thought, any road."

The sharp voice ran through Jan's head until she felt her own thoughts pressing back and struggling to burst out into words. She wanted to shout back at the voice. But she clenched her teeth, then said, quietly, "Thanks, Gran," and put down the phone.

Now, she knew why she was angry. She swung round at Dad where he stood at the foot of the stairs: "Did you hear that?"

His finger leapt to his lips. Her voice dropped.

"You heard what Gran said?"

He gestured upwards and turned to climb back to the bedroom. She followed and entered to find him sitting on the bed. His outdoor clothes were still strewn across it.

"Gran says Mum ran away from home, before when she was young."

He nodded. "Yes, I know."

"But she could be wandering about anywhere, Dad. Can't we go back to the police?"

His head lowered. "I have done, twice." He looked up. "And I've been down to the Salvation Army. They ask their people up and down to keep an eye open for missing persons."

"Oh Dad. Why didn't you tell me?"

"I couldn't. You looked so miserable. I hoped there might be some news. I didn't want to drag you around."

"But I can't go on like this. We've got to do something. Can't you tell Gran at Warby?"

His lips tightened.

"No, not yet. I don't want Gran to know, just yet."

From deep inside her mind, she dragged up the words:

"Dad, do you think that . . . ?"

But she could not complete her question. At first he seemed not to notice she had spoken, then he said, unwillingly:

"What's that, Jan?"

"Nothing, Dad."

He stared at her but did not press her to go on. There was something in his eyes, which she could not understand. For a second they faced one another and then both turned in silence to leave the room.

Days dragged by. At school she worked as though work were a drug, but got no relief. At home in the dead house, the evenings passed in silence. Kevin came straight home now, took his tea and went silently to his little room. The routine of their lives, shaped by Mum, went on.

But Mum was not there.

Then, one evening as she sat, head lowered over her books, not reading, but pressing her forehead to the cool smoothness of the page, the ringing of the phone lifted Jan from her seat. She threw herself to the stairs, but Dad was heading for the phone already. She watched him, listening and nodding. He looked up at her, the receiver still in his hand, and said in a loud whisper:

"It's the police. They want me to come. They've taken a woman out of the river. They don't know who she is."

Chapter 5

Jan, waiting in the car while her father went into the hospital, saw him come out with a dazed look on his face. She stared, trying to read his mind. He saw her and shook his head with a little smile on his face. The tenseness passed from inside Jan for a moment and her eyelids prickled with unshed tears. Then the familiar ache returned.

At school and in the shops, people spoke to her no longer. She strode by herself along Gorse Lane, walked the school corridors and wandered among the stacks in the supermarket, choosing without seeing. When her purse was empty, she asked Dad for more money, ignoring his anxious glances and muttered hints about "being careful". It did not seem to bother her that no one spoke to her. She was enough for herself and walked alone. As she passed the high, dark crumbling walls of the old people's home in Gorse Lane, she quickened her pace without thinking. In school assembly, the hundreds of faces around pressed close to her. There was a tightness in her head and her nerves seemed to be closer to her skin, as though a word or a touch would be too much to bear.

But the call to identify the dead woman seemed to spur her father to action again. One evening, when Kevin, glum but unprotesting, had been packed off to bed, there was a knock at the front door. Dad brought a man into the front room and they stayed there, talking for half an hour. From her bedroom, Jan heard their voices but could not tell what they were saying, but after the man was let out at the front door, she stopped her father on the stairs.

"Who's that, Dad?"

At first it seemed he would tell her to mind her own business, but then he looked embarrassed. He hesitated.

"It's someone who's helping me – us – find Mum."

"But, how?"

"Oh, he'll try and work out where she went that – Monday. Ask if anyone saw her."

"But I thought you didn't want us to talk to anyone about . . ."

"He's going to do it very discreetly."

Suddenly he sounded angry.

"I've got to do something, haven't I?"

She flinched at the words, then stood aside and let him go up to his room.

There were phone calls that next evening and the next, but Dad took them all, speaking low and covering the receiver with his cupped hand. He made phone calls, too, in the same way.

Jan began to listen at doors, to peer sideways into her parents' bedroom as she went along the landing, to sit still by her window in the evenings, watching the street, listening with breath held tight when the phone rang.

On Friday night, Dad decided that they should all drive down to the sea the next day. Jan made sandwiches and filled a Thermos flask. The weather was fine, and while Dad drove, she played "I spy" with Kevin. He was quick and his eyes, so like Mum's, sparkled with excitement as he guessed even the most difficult objects Jan chose. As Kev giggled and shouted in triumph, she saw in the mirror a little smile round Dad's lips. She sensed his pride and felt a twinge of irritation with them both.

While the two of them played at castles on the sand, Jan put on her swimsuit and wandered to the shore. The air was cold, the water colder. But on an impulse she waded in and flung herself forward in a low dive. She swam well and before exam pressures had crowded in on her had led her year team. To turn and roll in the water, to strike out and feel her body cut through it so smoothly, gave her a great feeling of freedom. She could drive on and on, the water bearing her up, no one in her way, no one holding her back.

"Jan! Jan! Come back!"

She jackknifed in the water as though turning in a race and threw the hair out of her eyes. Far away, on the almost empty beach, stood her father, wading up to his knees, waving. Little Kev jumped up and down by his side. She swam back strongly, but could feel all her limbs fill with fatigue that slowed her down and down. Her breath came with more difficulty, the shore line became hazy in her eyes. Suddenly she was swallowing water and coughing.

"Jan!"

She pushed down with her legs and touched bottom. Her knees buckled, she went forward and scrambled on all fours on the cold, wet sand.

Her father's hand raised her up. She felt his forearm muscles tense. He was strong. They walked up the beach. His trousers were stained to the knee with salt water.

"What were you doing, Jan?"

She stared at him.

"Just swimming, Dad."

"You were almost out of sight." He tried to joke. "I thought you weren't coming back."

"Oh, Dad."

They ate their sandwiches in an almost empty café on the front. Jan found her appetite had come back. She ate as greedily as Kev and the sandwiches were not enough to go round. Dad bought cake and ice cream and she was ready to have a second helping until she saw her father's lips tighten and his hand unconsciously feeling in his jacket pocket. He frowned over the bill, but said nothing to them.

In the afternoon they went to a Disney film, one of those stories with lots of knockabout action. They all laughed and Kev's face turned red with hiccuping. In the early evening Dad drove them back. Jan sat in the back seat with Kevin, who went to sleep in her arm, his head falling down into her lap, while she smoothed the sweat-damp hair out of his eyes. Back home she could not wake him, but lifted him from the car. Dad tried to take him, but she held Kev fast and carried him up the stairs to the bathroom. He stirred.

"Can I watch 'The Hulk', Mum?"

"We'll see, Kev love." She turned her head away.

In the bathroom, eyes closed, he swayed against her as she undressed and washed him. Boys' bodies were comic, she thought, not awkward like hers with its angles and bulges. She carried him, still naked, into the bedroom, slipped on his pyjamas and rolled him into bed. He was already asleep again. She bent and kissed him, switched off the light and went downstairs.

Dad was in the kitchen, drinking lager.

"Like one, Jan?"

She didn't really like beer, but she accepted. The sour-sweet liquid went down easily, though.

"Thanks, Dad. That was a nice day."

"Thanks for coping with Kev, love."

"Sorry about swimming off. I was coming back."

He did not answer. But as she turned to go upstairs to bed, later in the evening, he stood up awkwardly and kissed her good night. It was the first time he had done this since she was very small. She fell asleep the moment her body touched the bed.

She woke to the faint sound of voices. Putting on the Chinese pattern dressing-gown Mum had passed on to her earlier that year, still with its faint whiff of her scent, Jan went downstairs. The familiar, weary, inner ache had gone but she did not dare notice for fear it should return or there should be worse in its place.

Her brother sat in the kitchen pushing spoonfuls of soggy cereal into his mouth.

"Where's Dad?"

"Front room."

Jan swung open the front room door and was halfway in before she realized that Dad was not alone. Across from him seated on one of the dining chairs, raincoat still on, notebook in hand, was the man who had called at the house earlier in the week. He was speaking and Jan heard what he said before both he and her father stopped their conversation and turned to gape at her.

"No doubt about it, Mr Whitfield. The shop assistant in Barkways remembered quite clearly. She came in her everyday clothes, bought a complete new outfit and a travelling case, then got into a car that was waiting outside.

"The newspaper seller at the station saw her get out of a car and walk up to the barrier. There was a young feller with her, carrying her case."

Chapter 6

Jan backed out of the front room and ran quickly upstairs. Standing in front of the dressing-table mirror she saw her own face grey white, teeth pressing into the bottom lip. She sensed the pressure, but no pain. It seemed to her that even if blood came, it would not hurt.

She heard Tina Ellis's voice in the schoolyard.

"Our Mum cleared off six months back."

And her own aggressive answer.

"What are you talking about?"

A sudden feeling of shame, then a sickness in the stomach, then a wild wish to hide herself somewhere, came and went. She breathed in rapidly and paced about the room, trying to force the words out of her mind.

The front door slammed and she heard Dad call to Kevin.

"Get yourself washed, lad, and get your suit on."

"Hey, are we going to Gran's, Dad? Great."

Her brother's footsteps rattled on the stairs, followed by the heavier ones of his father. She met him on the landing.

"Dad!"

"Look, Jan. We'll talk tonight, when we get back from Warby."

"But, what are you going to say?"

"Don't worry. It'll be all right. Come on, you like going to Warby."

His voice was suddenly eager, as though he was already thinking about the trip. He turned into his own bedroom and she went back to hers. She got out her favourite dress, a deep-blue, three-quarter length, combed her hair (it was getting too long) and put on earrings. It was all done mechanically. You always got dressed up when you went to Warby.

Warby meant a big dinner, roast lamb and greens from the garden, trifle and as many sweets and chocolate as you could eat, until Mum frowned and shook her head. Then Granddad would say: "Come on, Val, they're only young once," and Mum would answer, "Ah, and fat ever after." The two of them would grin at each other. Granddad liked Mum, Jan knew.

As they drove up out of town and on to the moor road, Dad chatted to Kevin, pointing out curlew and snipe as they swooped over the mosses. And, "Look, Kev, that's a sparrow hawk." Alone in the back seat Jan could deal with her own thoughts, feeling the change within her as she fully grasped the meaning of the conversation she had blundered into earlier that morning. She considered herself as though she were someone else, like a doctor examining a patient. The sick feeling went. But inside her the dull, listless weight had vanished too. Her whole body seemed warily alive again. She smelled the spring breeze that drifted in through the partly open car window, took in the hills, slowly greening again as the snow retreated to the tops. Her mind separated things out once more, paused over them as though willing to think, interested in the difference between things she could bear and things she could not.

Mum was there again. Not home with them, but alive, somewhere out in the world. The notion brought a little wave of excitement, then a deeper pang. Mum wasn't away. She'd *gone* away, she'd "cleared off". She'd left them, Dad, Kev and Jan, gone somewhere without a word, just leaving a full fridge and a stocked-up larder. After all, Mum always saw to everything.

That was Mum. But who was this woman, buying herself a new outfit and a case and driving off to the station with a young feller? How young? Young like Peter? How old was Mum? Mum was – a woman.

Warby was an overspill area, a moor village with an old ruined mill, a battered chapel and a great circle of council houses, raw and orange-grey, to the horizon. Gran had never liked it, missing her old gossips from the town, but Granddad had a big garden and pottered to his heart's content, growing champion leeks and great crinkly winter cabbage.

Everything seemed the same as they drew up and the old couple came to the gate, meeting Kev with open arms as he tumbled like a plump puppy out of the car. They showed no surprise that Mum was not with them. What had Dad told them? Jan wondered, and the thought struck her like a dart – when had he realized, how long ago had he secretly made up his mind about why Mum

44

had gone? Then she pushed the thought away into that shadowed place at the back of her mind.

"Come on in, dinner's almost ready. Jan, love, you're looking peaky."

"She's not eating enough. She wants her ribs lining."

There was a great hug from Granddad that left her breathless, a quick peck from Gran and then they were in the cluttered front room with its slippery leather settee and its faint smell of mothballs.

"I'll take our Geoff down to the Weavers," said Granddad.

"All right, but it's on the table at one o'clock sharp."

Dad and Granddad went out.

"Can I see the whippets, Granddad?"

"Ah, off you go, but don't stick your fingers in the wire, lad. They're not vegetarians."

Now they were left alone, Gran and she.

"Come in the kitchen, Jan love. You can peel the apples for me."

The kitchen window looked out on the moors and Jan stood by the sink, taking in the view. She knew just then, with the new understanding she had gained this very day, why she hated the street and the narrow house Mum and Dad had bought. It had no horizon. No matter where you looked, brick and stone stood up to block out the view.

She felt Gran's brisk fingers tie an apron round her waist and picked up the coring knife.

"I've a nice recipe for apple crumble you can have, Jan love. There's a good many have asked me for it, but I don't give it out to all comers. I had it from my Gran, what d'you think of that?"

Jan heard Gran's voice, but only later that day, in the car going home, did she take in the words. Gran rattled on:

"Some folk are all for doing their shopping in one grand slam. Get the car out, off to the supermarket, come home weighed down like a packhorse. I always say, buy a bit every day, buy fresh, keep busy. I reckon they stick a penny or tuppence on everything at weekends.

"Hey, love, go easy on that knife. We shall have all core and no apple."

"Sorry, Gran."

"You've got good, strong fingers, and light, too. You should make good pastry. Course, you young women buy it all ready-made these days, don't you?"

Granddad and Dad passed by the kitchen window and Kevin came running in from the garden. Jan felt a pain in her chest. She had been holding her breath while Gran talked.

No one spoke over dinner. That was the unwritten law in Gran's house. But, over the apple crumble, Granddad, fiddling with his belt, to let out a notch, grinned at Jan.

"Well, Jan, how's the study going? Bi-ology is it, eh, and geography. And is it 'O' or 'A' levels, I always get those letters mixed up."

" 'O' level this summer, Granddad, the first exam's in a month's time. 'A' levels come in two years' time."

"Of course," put in Gran, "she could leave school this summer if she wanted. She's well gone sixteen."

"Eh, what?" said the old man. "Our Jan? No, she's a great scholar, she is. She could be a teacher, she could."

"Those houses cost a lot, you know, with that mortgage and all." Gran was glaring at Granddad now.

"I don't know why they had to buy that place, any road," said Granddad. "They had a perfectly good council flat."

The two old people had forgotten their guests now.

"Ah, but you don't get on in a council flat. Pay, pay, till they carry you out, like us." Gran leaned her elbows on the table, a sure sign that she was irritated. "They can sell their place and get a new one, when our Geoff's finished his course. They'll need a place they can invite folks to. You can't have lecturers and managers and such people home to a council flat."

"What the 'ell does that matter, woman? Can't our lad get on in the world without being posh, for God's sake?"

"Kevin, love, you can get down," snapped Gran.

Eyes wide, Kevin slipped from his chair and ran out into the garden. Jan's father got up from his chair and shut the door.

"Look, Mum, Dad, don't fall out over us. We're going to manage. That course'll be finished in a year's time and then I'll get more than I ever did in production, and prospects. It's just going to be tight, that's all."

Gran turned and looked at Jan.

"Our Jan'll help all she can, I'm sure. You have to do without some things in this life."

She smiled, but there was an edge to her words.

Granddad pushed back his chair.

"Come on, Jan. I'll walk you up to Borley Top. Put some colour in those cheeks."

47

"I was going to help Gran with the washing up."

"Give over, you can get enough of that at home. Come on lass, you take one dog, I'll take the other."

On the hillside beyond the houses, Grandad let the dogs go, tucked Jan's arm under his, and together they climbed slowly up the slope. To the west the sky was awash with a gentle pink. To the east the grey was shading into a darker blue.

"Hey up, lass. Soon be summer. We haven't seen you up here half enough this past winter. When your exams are over, you'll have to come up more. Don't wait for your Dad to bring you, he's got enough on his plate. Bring Kev up on the bus."

"Thanks, Granddad."

At the top of the ridge, they looked down into distant hills and valley folds. Some were already hidden in mist. Jan realized that Granddad was speaking to her.

"Jan, love. There'll be a reason for it. There will, you know. It won't be just like it seems."

Jan choked.

"Don't, Granddad, please."

"All right, chuck." The old man slapped his hands against his coat.

"Let's turn about then. It's a bit parky up here."

He whistled up the dogs and they walked back without saying a word. But as they were about to leave the hill and walk down the estate track, the old man suddenly said fiercely:

"There's two words I can't abide and never could and I've heard 'em all my life. That's 'do without'. Why should we? Who says we should?"

The other three were waiting as they came up to the

house, Dad and Kevin in coats and scarves. Gran kissed Jan lightly on her cheek and slipped something into her pocket.

"Look after yourself, our Jan."

Kev tugged at Jan's sleeve.

"Can I sit in the back with you, Jan?"

He scrambled on to the seat and arranged himself cat-like with his head against her. Before the car had gone half a mile down the moor road, he had dozed off. Jan felt in her pocket. There were three pieces of paper, folded together, two pound notes and the recipe for apple crumble. She gazed out of the car window at the falling darkness. What was going to happen to them? What was going to happen to her?

Gran was quite sure. Jan was going to take her mother's place, look after Dad and Kev, because Mum wasn't coming back. Granddad was sure things weren't what they seemed.

Who could she believe? Who was this woman they called Mum, all these years? And where, where was Mum?

Chapter 7

When Kev was safely in bed, Jan sat with her father in the kitchen. He did not meet her glance, but sat quietly as if waiting for her to accuse him. But she was tired. The words came out unwillingly.

"Dad, did you know – all the time?"

"What d'you mean?" he said, half-heartedly.

"I mean, about why Mum went. I mean, you told Gran, you must have told her something . . . even before that – that bloke came and said about the station and Mum going off with . . ."

"I had to tell Gran something."

"But, why not me, Dad, why not me?"

His hand went up to his mouth.

"You – I didn't want – I was hoping it would turn out . . ."

"Dad," her voice was low, "did you know before?"

"No," he spoke harshly, bitterly. "She never said ought. Everything seemed normal. She never said . . ."

He jerked up from the table, took his cup and threw the tea into the sink.

"Shall I make a fresh cup, Dad?"

He shook his head and sat down again.

"Look, Jan, we've got to manage somehow. We've got to carry on. We've got to get things straight, somehow . . . I mean, there's the money."

"What money, Dad?"

"Hey, you know. The housekeeping money. It's in a mess. I've been giving you bits and pieces all the time. I'll have to give you a fixed amount every week. I mean, well, it used to come out of her wages and now . . ."

He tapped on the table as if he were trying to convince himself.

"If it won't stretch, Jan, we'll just have to do without."

Do without, Jan thought to herself. So soon.

That first week, though, the money had all gone by Thursday and she had used Gran's two pounds to tide them over. Against her will, she began to follow the prices in the supermarket, even found herself chatting about them with fellow shoppers. They were all friendly, extra friendly, it seemed to her, with her newly sharpened wits. And her eyes and hearing seemed sharper, too. She noticed more what people said and did. The woman next door stopped offering to do the shopping for her. The lady at the cash point in the supermarket had stopped asking how her mother was.

It was as though, for all the family's trying to keep things to themselves, everyone knew what was going on. If they didn't know, they'd guessed, and people always guessed right in the end. They knew she wouldn't answer their questions. They knew why she wouldn't answer and they knew that she knew.

That was the strange thing. Now that they seemed to

know Mum had walked out on them, it was all in order. No mystery, no interest, just life. They talked to Jan as though she was Mum, Mum as she used to be, not that woman who'd taken the train out of town with a young feller carrying her case.

Jan noticed, too, that the supermarket lady and the manager were up to something. There was an edge to their backchat. How old were they? She must be older than him, her hair must be grey under that rinse, his was black and smooth. This must be going on all the time, only she, Jan, the bright girl, the scholar who learnt so many things in books, she knew nothing about it.

At school she noticed, out of the corner of her eye, Sharon hanging around Pete and his friends at the entrance to the sixth form block – compensation prize for him perhaps. No, that had a touch of the miaow about it. Good luck to her, good luck to him, she told herself and did not know if she believed it or not.

Now she saw more clearly the concerned look on the face of Miss Maudesley. She went to her, smiling brightly and asking about certain books she needed for her final weeks' studies. She noticed the warm smile suddenly appear on her tutor's face and thought, carelessly, how easily you could please people, or upset them, just like children.

There was comfort in work. She drew up plans for each evening, one subject a day. She worked out how many hours she had left, which subjects she should take first, made a chart and stuck it on the wall of her bedroom. And she began to go straight from the school to the local library, where the reference room was warm, and when the old men had gone home for the day she could find an empty table in a corner and work for an hour before going home. Left to himself, Kevin began to sneak into the neighbour's kitchen again, and she would find him there curled up, sticky-faced in front of the television set. She'd have a cup of tea with the woman next door and chat lightly about this and that.

She left the house-cleaning and the washing to the weekends and pretended not to hear Dad's subdued grumbles when clean shirts were not to hand in midweek. This was how Jan did things and if people didn't like it, well, they could do the other.

"Another cup of tea, Dad? Look, you haven't finished the first one yet, have you?"

It came as a shock to her to find, one evening as she sat over her books in the library, that she was filled with a sudden, desperate misery. She stared around her without seeing, with that familiar stinging under her eyelids. But she could not cry. She knew that if she could weep, she would do so right there and then in the reference library, right under the silence notice. She would sob and choke and wail and let the tears run down her face on to the page and sniff and wipe her nose with her hand. But none of that happened and all she did was stare grey-faced and dry-eyed at the wall like someone who had found themselves in a strange town.

It was half past six and the librarian waited to close the reference room. Jan packed up her things and hurried home. She had never been later than six before and always got home and called Kev in before Dad arrived. As she hurried up the street, shoes clumping in the evening quiet, the neighbour's door was open. Light streamed out and the telly in the kitchen beyond boomed away. There were voices, hers and a man's. That was funny. She had men visitors, they usually came earlier in the day, like the tally man who came after breakfast for his £1 weekly sub, and took so long to collect it.

But it was Dad, sitting there in the neighbour's kitchen, chatting, having a cup of tea and a fag. She saw this in a split second before passing on, noisily opening their own front door and going in. Dad came in with Kev five minutes later and sat down to the cup of tea she had made.

"Just picked up Kev. I think he likes next door's telly better than ours."

"Oh, yes, Dad?"

"What's up with you, Jan?"

"Oh, nothing, Dad, just month end, I think."

His eyes widened slightly, but he said:

"Tell you what, Jan. I'll make tea. You go and lie down."

She walked into the bathroom. The cabinet was full to bursting. Mum had bought three of everything, soap tablets, bottles of shampoo, packets of Tampax . . .

That night, which was Friday, after Kevin was in bed, Dad got out his new suit and went down to the club. It was the first time since . . . the first time in weeks, Jan noted. Left in the house unable to study, she watched a TV series she had given up months before as mindless. She found it enjoyable, watched it through, then the next programme and finally went to sleep in the armchair during the political broadcast. She woke to the front door closing, as Dad came in. It was nearly midnight. He walked, picking his steps with care and whistling through his teeth, up the stairs. At the front room door she looked after him. He stood, swaying slightly, halfway up the staircase.

"Good night, Dad."

"Go- night, love."

On Monday afternoon she stayed on in the library again, deep in her books. Someone's shadow fell over them. She looked up, confused.

"Sorry, I didn't know it was closing time, already," she apologized.

"Get off, Jan, it's hardly opening time."

She blinked in the light. Peter sat on the opposite side of the table.

"Oh, hello."

"Brilliant," he answered. " 'Hello' she says. I ask her a vitally important question and two years later she says 'Oh, hello'."

She blushed.

"I'm sorry."

"I'm impressed."

"What d'you mean?"

He leaned across the table. "If you want an answer to that question, you'll have to buy me a coffee."

She felt for her handbag.

"Don't be daft," he said. "I'll buy you a coffee."

The coffee bar was next door. Just a brief sensation of the cool evening and then they were in warmth and bright light again, looking at one another across the table.

"Well?" he said.

"Well, what?" She began to feel foolish.

"You are out of this galaxy. You were going to ask me what impressed me."

"Oh, yes?"

"Hey, you're not doing this on purpose, just to put me on, are you?"

"No," she was surprised at the indignation in her voice.

He cleared his throat. "Stand by for a press announcement."

She smiled, put her head on one side: "Shall I take notes?"

He waved a hand. "Not necessary. This will be unforgettable. Ha hm. In his long career, Mr Peter Carey said last night, and I quote, 'I have been told no, occasionally. I have been told, rather more frequently, yes, but never has anyone told me "I'll let you know" and then not spoken to me for two years.'"

"It wasn't two years, it was four weeks."

"What's the odds? It might have been for ever if I had not relaxed my rules concerning ladies who play hard to get, so far as to pursue you into the public library."

"I'm not playing hard to get." Her voice was sharp. "I've had other things on my mind."

"Oh, and what other things could possibly . . ." his voice dropped as he saw her face. He put a hand out and took hers. "Sorry. Just me being funny." He went on, hastily: "I mean, apart from – other things, if you *had* said something to me, what would you have said?"

She gave his hand a squeeze and drew hers back.

"Apart from other things, yes."

"Oh, magic. Now as the Indian chief said: You know how – I want to know when."

"Well, I've got my exams."

"So have I, but I have to let it all go one evening in the week."

"OK, so you say."

"Friday, Jan?"

She nodded. "What shall we do?"

"Don't tempt me to reply," he answered. "Tell you what, let's meet here, seven o'clock, and invent something. Agreed?"

"Agreed."

He leant over the table as if to kiss her. But she turned her head slightly and he gave up the attempt. Funny, she'd seen women do this in films, but she'd no idea it was so easy.

She got home to find Kevin in bed and Dad sitting black-browed at the kitchen table.

"Look at this," he said. "The little blighter had even opened it on the way home from school."

This was a letter from Kevin's teacher asking for his parents to come and see her. His behaviour had been "unusual" for some little time past. Now it had become "almost impossible".

"When are you going?" she asked.

"Thursday. I'll get off early."

"Do you want me with you?"

"Better not. It does rather underline that . . ."

She nodded. "Do you reckon Kevin knows Mum's not . . . ?"

He snorted. "Who doesn't, round here? And the rest can put two and two together and make five, even seven-year-olds in the juniors. We're a broken home, Jan, and they all know about broken homes." He put on a prissy voice. "It is an established fact that more than one million children are from single-parent households."

"It's not funny, Dad."

"I didn't bloody say it was. Listen, Jan, did you know I've been up two nights running with that lad, having nightmares and howling for his Mum?"

"I didn't know that, Dad."

His voice softened. "I know. You're at the front, my room's next to his. And you've been sleeping like the dead this past week."

"Maybe he's watching too much telly. He's in next door a lot," said Jan.

"Hm, are you ready to come home early from where-ever it is you go after school, to get him in? I can't get home any earlier. No," he went on, "I don't think it's the telly. It's something he wants and he can't have."

"Dad," her voice was low. "If you knew where Mum was would you try and get her back?"

He stood up with such force that the chair fell back on the floor.

"You must be joking, Jan, you must be joking."

Chapter 8

As if by agreement, Jan and Pete did not speak to one another at school next day, just a nod and a half wave across the yard when he rode in on his bike. Not that it made any difference. Everyone knew. They always did. As she came to her desk at registration there was a sudden hush all round her and then whispering began. She looked round and it stopped, but she found herself exchanging glances with Sharon. In Sharon's glance there was nothing but hostility. Jan shrugged and turned round. When she ignored Pete that didn't suit. Now he was dating her, that didn't suit either. Well, it could do the other.

That afternoon, instead of going to the library, she hurried home and collected Kevin from next door, made him tea, read to him for a while and, when he tired of that, sat with him watching the telly. It was a programme she remembered from her own childhood, but now with different people in it. It all seemed far away from her. She looked at Kev, thumb in mouth, staring at the white square. It couldn't be the same for him, ever.

But next day she'd shopping to do and left him next door. "Don't bother, dear," said the neighbour. "I expect his Dad'll stop by and pick him up later on."

Jan found the supermarket almost empty and collected her shopping in such a rush that she was at the check point before she realized. Two people sprang apart as she came into view round the nearest shelf stack. The manager walked over to the exit whistling and the check-out lady smoothed her hair delicately and turned to her with cheeks slightly reddened.

"Hello, dear. Any news of your mother yet?"

The effrontery of the question took her aback. Yet it sounded so innocent.

In the split second while she pondered whether to ignore it or not, someone spoke up behind her.

"How much is that mixed dried fruit, please? It's not marked."

Behind her was old Mrs Elsom from next door, her mouth pursed.

The checkout lady hastily consulted her cards, while Jan put down her basket by the cash register. Outside, she held the plate glass door open for the old woman, who came out stooping from the weight of her shopping. Mrs Elsom was old and weather-beaten like her husband. In fact, they could have been brother and sister. She wore her white hair in a net like women used in the 1940's, her old grey coat was missing two buttons and dark brown stockings hung wrinkled on bow legs. But she stepped out in a sprightly way, and Jan noticed now, for the first time, that she had a sweet smile.

She took one of the old woman's shopping bags and they walked slowly back to the street. Jan remembered how the old man had offered her potatoes and she had stupidly said no. Now she took the chance to apologize. Mrs Elsom wagged her head.

"Not to worry, love. He doesn't mind. He's always offering potatoes, here, there and everywhere. Blessed if I know why we grow so many. Three hundredweight last autumn. How can we eat all them? I asked him. Where am I going to keep them?"

Then she laughed.

"Still, it keeps him out of mischief. Not that we get up to much mischief at our time of life, worse luck." She nudged Jan.

At the street door, they paused a while. Next door's TV was belting out. The old woman wrinkled her nose.

"Some people . . ." She put her hand on Jan's sleeve.

"Tell you what. You come in now, we'll have a cup of tea and I'll let you have those potatoes. You'll be doing us a favour. Then we'll nip down to the plot and I'll cut you a nice spring cabbage. My Joe likes a nice crisp cabbage. I expect your Dad does as well."

She took the handles of her shopping bag from Jan's hand and pulled at her fingers. "Come on, love. The boy'll be all right."

Inside the small kitchen, identical to that in Jan's house, but seeming smaller, darker, more crowded, old Mrs Elsom swiftly made tea. She tumbled digestive biscuits on to a flower-patterned plate and chatted all the while, answering herself most of the time. Gratefully, Jan kept silent. Her thoughts drifted away and she began to think about Pete. Blokes were funny. First she'd put him off. She'd kept quiet because she was upset. Then Sharon was hanging about and she wasn't going to start a competition over any boy. She'd kept quiet, as well, because she didn't see why anyone should want to go out with her. Suddenly she saw herself from the outside, red hair flying, big nose sticking out like a ship's figurehead, heavy bosom wagging as she ran, long legs flying and shoes clopping away. Did blokes ever look at themselves, and wonder what girls saw in them? Pete seemed to know he was good-looking. Or else he didn't care. Blokes were always looking out at things, girls were always looking in at themselves.

"That was a deep sigh, love. Am I boring you with all this nattering?" Mrs Elsom put down her cup.

"Come on, let's go to the plot. Look, it's just gone five. Plenty of time. It's only ten minutes."

The allotments were on a wide sweep of waste land, further down the railway line, with the river running by at the end. One side was bounded by a tree-lined ditch and the Elsoms' plot was at the bottom, in the shade of the trees.

"Lots of things we can't grow so well down here. But the trees and bushes keep the worst of the frost off."

As they walked on the narrow path by the side of the plot, there was a rustling sound among the undergrowth by the ditch. Jan started.

"Rabbits," said Mrs Elsom. "Our Joe's always saying he'll catch one for supper. I tell him he's too slow to catch cold. But he's really too soft-hearted. Won't even do anything about those pigeons, and they eat more cabbage than we do."

The old woman bent with a tiny knife she had drawn

out of her pocket and quickly cut two plump cabbages, which she handed to Jan. She straightened up.

"Oh, my back." Her eyes narrowed. "There's more than rabbits down under those trees some days, I can tell you. You'd be surprised at what goes on, ah, and who's doing it. No names, no pack drill, my Joe says, but some people should watch it."

They walked slowly back and Jan knocked on her neighbour's open street door.

"Come in," came the call from the kitchen. She could see Kev curled up in a broken-down armchair, eyes glued on the box, and the woman's two sons, older than Kev. They eyed her up and down as she walked in. Their mother sat by the table, feet up on a kitchen stool, curlers in hair, fag in mouth.

"Oh, it's you, Jan. I thought it might be your father. He sometimes drops in these days. Still I expect he's late with a lecture. They put them through it on that training course, don't they?"

"Kevin love, it's time to come back, now." Jan spoke sharply and Kevin's face took on a sulky look.

"Ah, poor lamb. Let him watch the rest of the programme. It's nearly finished. Let 'em enjoy themselves while they can."

She stood up from the chair. "Come and sit down next door if you don't want to watch that old rubbish."

The front room was expensively furnished, but unused and cold. There was a blanket and sheet spread out over the settee. The woman whipped the blanket and sheet away with a quick movement, dropped them behind a chair and smiled boldly at Jan.

63

"I sometimes like a lie down in the afternoon, after lunch, like." She sat down and waved for Jan to do the same.

"Look, I can call you Jan, can't I? We know each other a bit better, now. You can call me Sandra, that'll make it easier."

She looked at Jan, eyebrows raised.

"You think I'm after your Dad, don't you?"

Jan's mouth opened, but no words came out.

Sandra went on: "Look, love, would you like a drink? I've got some nice sherry. I know a traveller . . ."

Jan shook her head.

"Well, I do fancy your Dad a bit. What's wrong with that? You think I'm as old as the hills, don't you? Well, I'm thirty-six, and your Dad's thirty-seven.

"I know more than that about him, anyway. He used to work on the assembly line at Bonner's with my Frank. In fact, we came here first and you moved here after us. I've always had a soft spot for your Dad, though I don't think he was ever bothered – then. It might be different now, of course. Though I was always very careful, so as not to upset Val, your Mum.

"Of course, my Frank, he was never careful. He fancied Val and the world knew about it. He'd as much tact as a bull in a china shop. Anything in skirts he'd be after it. He's probably the same, wherever he is now, the pig. And he usually got what he was after."

Sandra stopped and looked quickly at Jan. Jan stared back in silence and Sandra went on:

"But he was wasting his time with your Mum, love. She didn't want to know. The only ones who were really bothered were your Dad and me. It was a big mistake living next door to one another, I always reckoned. I mean, when you live a bit away from each other you can stay friends. When you're on top of one another, it's got to go this way or that. So, in the end we weren't on speaking terms, even after my Frank took off. I think your mother reckoned we were as bad as one another. And maybe she's right. I've learnt a thing or two since he left home."

Sandra crossed and uncrossed her legs on the settee. If she noticed how still Jan was, she seemed to take it as an invitation to say more.

"He walked out overnight. Never said a word. Took every bit of cash in the house and all our suitcases and even some of my dresses for his latest bird. He'd have had me out of here, too, if he could, but he slipped up there. I paid the mortgage and the house was in my name and as long as I keep the repayments up, Old Nick himself can't have me out."

She pointed to a corner table, where a sewing machine stood under a cloth cover.

"That's my best friend. I can knock up more with that in three days than most of those poor cows at Cartwright's can pull down in a week. I've got my own house, I've got my own money and the rest of them can go to Halifax."

Sandra bent forward.

"I'll give you some advice, too, Jan. Please yourself what you do with it. The men have it their way, because they pay their way, they come and go as they like and we silly bitches sit there and wait for 'em. Well, I play the game their way. I have them in, if I like them. I show 'em the door if I don't. If they don't like it, they can lump it.

What they have I take. I take them for all I can get. That's the name of the game."

There was a knock on the street door. Sandra rose and patted her hair.

"That'll be your father, Jan dear. Kevin love, come on," she called.

Chapter 9

A gentle feeling of warmth and excitement took Jan through the week, growing a little each day until at times it filled every part of her body. She would find herself halfway down Gorse Lane on the way home from school, doing hopscotch steps on the pavement, then stopping to look round to see if anyone had spotted her. Not that it made any difference. A few weeks ago she had crept from day to day, hoping no one would see poor Jan and no one would know anything about her. Now she knew that they all knew. She was Jan, the girl from a broken home, whose Mum had walked out on them. Poor Jan, poor cow. And she didn't give a toss. She knew a lot more now than she knew last month. She was going with Peter Carey. So you can stick that . . .

A woman, wearily pushing a pram along the road, turned round sharply and Jan realized she must have spoken aloud. She ran like a little girl down the road, past the looming wall of the old folks' home, and did not draw breath until she had dived into the gloomy safety of her own street.

There she stopped a split second, her heart beating faster. The car was parked in front of their house. Dad was home early.

Was he in next door? Well, she shrugged, so what? She almost spoke aloud. But there was hurt inside her. Then she remembered, it was Thursday and Dad had been to school to see about Kev. She had to stop jumping to conclusions about people. She hesitated outside the front door. The last thing she needed in her present mood was a heavy family scene.

She walked past the front door and towards the other end of the street, across the parade, where the shops were, and down a side street towards the river path. Overhead the sky was blue and the day had been warm, though just now a cool little breeze was blowing off the grey-brown water. Jan breathed in deeply and walked idly along the edge of the waste ground, the river on one side of her and the allotments on the other. As she drew near the tree-lined ditch that bordered the Elsoms' plot, she heard rustling in the grass. Rabbits? She hadn't seen one in years. Laying her bag on the path, she tiptoed slowly forward to look between the bushes.

And stopped.

A couple of yards away from her at the side of a clump of rough grass, lay a blue handbag, as though someone had dropped it. A rather stylish bag, thought Jan. It must have an address inside, so that she could return it. She bent forward to pick it up and then stopped, half bent over, eyes and mouth wide open. Attached to the hand-bag was a long, blue, leather strap and curled in the loop were a woman's fingers, thin, white and veined, with two ornate stoned rings on the third finger. Jan's hand went to her mouth in a swift gesture of fear. A body?

Then the fingers curled, clenched and unclenched, shifted to one side, dragging the handbag with them. As they did so the rustling sound in the bushes grew louder. There was whispering and a high-pitched giggling. Jan drew back two or three paces to where her own bag lay on the path. As she did she heard a woman's anxious voice:

"Hey up, there's somebody coming."

And a man's voice, hoarse and grumbling:

"Is there hellaslike. Give over, you're putting me off my stroke."

Jan snatched up her bag and ran, stifling her laughter. Once safely away, she let it go in great shouts. The tears streamed down her cheeks and her laughter turned to hiccups. She stopped and leaned against a wall in the nearest street and drew in deep breaths to recover. The voices were unmistakeable. It was the prim saleslady and the supermarket manager. Hey, and it wasn't even early closing today. They must have slipped out smartish while one of the girls from the cold meat counter took a turn on the checkout. Perhaps if she were to go to the supermarket before they closed tonight, she'd find madam there patting her hair and passing the time of day with the customers, giving them the latest gossip.

Jan hugged herself. She'd get a laugh out of this with Pete. Or would she? Did she know him well enough to share that kind of joke? You could never tell with people. Look at milady in the supermarket.

She stopped abruptly at the corner of their street. That woman was older than Mum, but she thought nothing of having it away with her fancy man. Before Jan could close her thoughts to it, a picture of Mum flashed into her mind, not Mum as she knew her but another one, dressed in different clothes, hanging on to a bloke's arm, turning down a side street, sending a quick glance behind her as they quickened their pace, hurrying out of sight. Mum without Kev, without Dad, without Jan, a woman with a bloke, any bloke, a woman . . . So clear was the image that for a second the street she was in vanished, and she was nowhere. Dizzy, she stopped and leaned against a wall. Then she saw a yard away, her own door. Dad and Kev were in the front room watching children's television. Kev had a big ice cream which he was steadily stuffing into his mouth. Dad had a cup of tea in his hand. When he heard Jan at the door, he came out.

"Cup of tea in the pot, Jan."

He sat down in the kitchen as she poured out her cup of tea, lightly swinging the kitchen door shut as he did.

"Kev's teacher reckons he's very disturbed," he said quietly.

She shrugged. "Not really surprising, is it, Dad?"

"She reckons he's bottling it up at home and letting it out at school. He's been a real little devil by all accounts."

"What can we do, Dad? He wants his Mum and he can't have her. So do I."

He stared at her with a quick drawing-in movement of the lips.

"Ah, but we've got to manage, haven't we, love? For one thing, we've got to see he's not left in the house on his own, particularly not late evenings. He's started waking up, having nightmares. I told you that, Jan."

"Well, he's hardly ever left alone. There's usually one

or other of us here, isn't there, Dad?"

He put his hand flat down on the table.

"We've got to make sure there's always someone here, you or I, Jan. He's too young to cope with this."

"Dad," she burst out, suddenly remembering. "Tomorrow, I shall be out in the evening. I've got an arrangement . . ."

He frowned.

"Well, I'm sorry, Jan, but Friday's my night out. You know that. It always has been. In fact, it's the only night I do have at the club. They've asked me to come down other nights, for the darts team, but I've always said no."

"But, Dad," her voice rose. "I can't just . . ."

"You'll have to, Jan. You'll just have to let whoever it is know," he glanced sharply at her, "and fix another night. Look, Jan, any other night than Friday."

"Well, I can't."

"Well, you'll have to. It's no good telling me on Thursday night I've got to cancel my club night."

"And it's no good telling me on Thursday night, I've got to cancel my d-"

"Can't your friend come round here and have a cup of coffee instead?"

"Not really."

"Oh, like that? Anyway, Jan. We'll just have to talk things over at the beginning of the week in future. But right now, no. Friday's my night."

She marched from the kitchen and up the stairs, bringing her feet down with great force at each step. Inside the bedroom, she took her coat and flung it across the room, then hurled herself on to the bed. Bloody Kev, Bloody

71

Dad. She began to say "Bloody Mum", then stopped, as though she didn't know how to say it.

There was a tap at her door. Dad stood outside.

"Listen, Jan, I'd be quite willing to go turns, Friday evenings with you – if I had notice. But not like this."

"Oh, forget it," she shouted, the sound of her voice pleased her by its force. "Forget it."

There was silence a moment, then.

"Jan," he said again, speaking softly as though she were a little girl in a temper.

Heaving herself from the bed, she swung open the door. To his astonished face, she shouted once more, "Forget it" and slammed the door again.

She threw herself back on the bed and waited for an angry answer from her father. But no word came, only the sound of his tiptoeing away into his own room.

On her way to school next day, she pondered how to put it to Peter. What would he say? Ignoring him once might seem smart. But putting him off again would be more than a joke. It would finish altogether something which had given her that good feeling again for the first time in months.

But Pete wasn't there. A friendly and rather curious sixth form lad told her he had not turned up that day.

He grinned.

"I shouldn't worry. He always does this to his birds."

She turned her back on him quickly and walked away as though she could cancel out the words by doing this. At lunchtime she went out to the corner phone booth. For once it was working, but there was a queue. Later in the afternoon she slipped out between periods and went to the phone box again, hastily thumbing through the phone book. There were four Careys. The first one was an old woman, deaf as a post. The next two did not answer. The fourth was engaged. She flung down the receiver.

As she rushed back into school she ran into Miss Maudesley at the classroom door and threw a hasty word of apology into her puzzled face. The rest of the afternoon crawled by. She heard nothing of the lesson and the words in her books made no sense to her. Her head and face grew warm and flushed as though she had 'flu, her teeth chewed one corner of her lip until it was sore.

At the end of the day, the queue had formed again outside the phone box. Furiously impatient, she took off down Gorse Lane at a run, nearly knocking two girls over by the school gate.

"You know what's wrong with her, don't you?"

But she was away down the lane, coat open, legs flying, heart beating. In her own road she plucked the door key from her bag as she ran, dropped it into the gutter, bent to pick it up, swearing, and burst into the house, sending the door crashing against the passage wall. Once again she looked through the phone book. Once again she dialled the three Careys, giving the deaf old lady the benefit of the doubt. Two of them answered. One grunted, "wrong number" and hung up. The second was a relation, who wanted to chat, but who finally confirmed that the fourth number was indeed Peter's.

But Pete's number did not answer. She rang again and again and later, in desperation, rang every few minutes.

Kevin came in and pushed past her in the hall as she

73

leaned, still in her outdoor clothes, by the open front door, clutching the phone now slippery with sweat. At last she gave up and went to make tea. Dad arrived home, bringing a box of chocolates which he put down silently beside her on the table. She did not look at him and they finished the meal without speaking to one another.

Jan went out, tried once more to phone Peter and then went upstairs to her room and sat with her books. After a while Dad came up and went into his room. Drawers opened and shut, the wardrobe door creaked. She heard him begin to whistle, a tuneless blowy sound like a small boy making his first attempt. He was in a good mood, she could tell. Was he meeting someone? What was Mum doing right now? Was she getting dressed and made up to go out? Where did she live? Was it a house (his house), or a flat, or room? Was she enjoying herself? Did she think of them?

Dad went downstairs calling to Kev.

"You'll be a good lad now. There's some popcorn in the front room you can have while you watch your programme. Remember, you go to bed when Jan tells you. Don't worry, there'll be someone here all the time. Jan'll be with you."

Kevin's voice came back sulkily.

"How do I know she won't go off? She's been ringing up her . . ."

Jan rushed out of her bedroom in outrage, but Dad was quietening Kev down, saying guiltily,

"That's enough now." He raised his voice.

"Jan, I'm off. See you . . ."

"See you." She bit back the words, "Have a nice

time." The door slammed, the car started and he was gone. From the front room came the sound of the television. Jan wandered into the hall and idly tried the phone again. It was engaged. Excited, she tried again and again. At last she was through.

"Peter?"

"No, this is Mrs Carey. I'm afraid Peter's out. Goodness knows where he's gone to, or who with for that matter." Mrs Carey giggled and Jan gritted her teeth. "I can't remember half their names, you know. Shall I give him a message? Well, shall I say who called? All right, dear, better luck next time."

In her agitation, Jan walked halfway up the stairs and then down into the kitchen. She picked up the chocolate box and climbed back to her room. Kneeling on the floor she dug out a pile of Chalet School stories she had not looked at since she was twelve, and began to read, mechanically sticking the chocolates one by one into her mouth. When the box was empty, she went down to the kitchen, opened the fridge, took out the single can of lager from the shelf and retired again to her room. An hour passed as she sipped the beer and turned the pages, putting one paperbacked volume aside and taking up another.

The sound of television changed as the news came on. She started and looked at her watch, then called downstairs to Kevin. There was no answer. She found him lying fast asleep, his face buried in the crushed popcorn packet. Heaving him up like a sack of potatoes she dragged him upstairs, wiped his face with a flannel and put him quickly to bed. The evening was almost gone.

Downstairs she changed channels and settled down to watch a thriller series. Her eyes began to smart and she half closed them.

"This night we come a soul-caking
Good night to you . . ."

From the pavement outside the front room window came a strange, piping, mock childish voice.

"And we hope you will remember,
That it's soul-caking time."

The front door rattled.

"Fol-i-dee, fol-i-di, fol-i-iddle-i-do."

Jan leapt up angrily, ran to the front door and snatched it open.

Outside, his hand outstretched to knock again, mouth wide open in mid-chorus, shirt collar gaping over half-knotted tie, black hair falling over his impudent eyes, stood Peter.

Chapter 10

"Peter!"

"Up with your kettles, down with your drums.
Give us an answer and then we'll be gone."

She took hold of his sleeve and pulled him indoors.

"You'll have half the street out."

The movement brought them close together in the hall. He kissed her. Happily she clung to him. He kissed her again, longer and more hungrily, stopping her breath. She pushed him away and shut the door. They looked at one another. His face was flushed. He had been drinking, she realized, though the beer she had drunk prevented her from smelling it on his breath. She led him down the passage into the kitchen. Why she did it she couldn't think, unless by some cautious instinct. He didn't seem to mind. He was in an amiable, nonsensical mood.

She sat him down at the kitchen table and put the kettle on. He rested his elbows on the table top and watched her move to and fro as if he saw her only hazily. She put the teacups down and filled them, then sat down herself.

"Pete, I'm sorry."

"I shall treasure those three words – 'Pete, I'm sorry'."

"Oh, shut your face." Her relief at seeing him made her aggressive.

"I shall treasure those four words. 'Oh, shut your face.' Your face shut. Your shut face. Face your shut."

"Pete, stop it. You'll say something you shouldn't."

He stopped, spoke soberly. "Where were you?"

"Oh, Pete, I've tried to reach you all day." She explained what had happened, the phone calls. He grinned.

"Mum's a bit of a pain sometimes." He shifted his chair round to her side of the table and put his arm round her, reaching under her arm. She moved away slightly. He changed his tactics, took her face between his hands and kissed her deeply, wetly.

"You'll knock my tea over."

He picked up his own cup and drank deeply.

"I will admit, I thought to myself – Jan's done it on me again. Hung me out to dry. I sat there, drinking that crummy coffee till it turned my insides. Then I went for a drink."

"But, why didn't you phone?"

"I thought I might get the brush off again."

"Pete!"

"Then I thought, I'll go round and embarrass her."

"You didn't!"

"I thought I had."

"You're daft, you know."

"Ah, but handsome with it. Let's go in the front room."

On the settee he slid off his jacket, unfastened his tie

and pulled her towards him. His hands were gentle, but she suspected he could be strong and rough. She let him kiss her but her mind was not on it. After a moment he let her go.

"Sorry, Pete, I've just been so fed up today."

He nodded.

"Look, Pete, can't we make it another evening next week. I'm stuck in on Fridays."

He stuck out his underlip, looked stubborn. Then he grinned slyly.

"Hey, no sweat. I could come round here, couldn't I?" He looked quickly at her. "I won't go to the pub first, promise. Tell you what, for another. I'll help you with your revising, if you like – for a bit, anyway." He raised his eyebrow.

"Would you, Pete?" He grinned at her eagerness.

"Yeah, if you can't beat the 'O' levels, join 'em."

"Thanks, Pete. You're sweet."

She kissed him and relaxed in his arms. Relief and tiredness made her drowsy. Then her eye noted the time on her wristwatch. She sprang up.

"Dad'll be here in a minute."

He leapt about wildly. "Quick, the back door, the window, the balcony, a rope ladder! My horse awaits." He ran to and fro and she collapsed in laughter. But he left quietly, giving her a friendly kiss and hug as he left.

"You're a funny girl, Jan."

Slowly, happily, she climbed the stairs, undressed and lay on the bed. Drawing a sheet over her, she drifted off to sleep.

Then she was awake again. The light was on, the door

open. Her father stood in the doorway, one hand on the door frame, the other holding something. Hazily, through her sleep-clogged thoughts, Jan realized that it was Peter's tie.

Her father was speaking to her, but she could not grasp what he said. But his grey eyes now stood out black in a white face. As she understood at last, she struggled from the bed, pulling the sheet round her.

"It's Peter's."

"Peter who?"

For a moment, child-like, she was about to refuse to say. Then her anger gave her dignity. She answered calmly.

"Peter Carey. From school. I was going to meet him tonight, but I couldn't."

The reminder of their earlier argument angered him more.

"So, you brought him round here?"

"No, he came to see why I didn't turn up."

"Oh, he did. We'll see about that. What's their phone number?" He half-turned to go downstairs. His movements were unsteady. Jan heard her own voice, firm, but cool.

"Dad, give over. It's gone midnight."

He rounded, his fingers slipping on the doorjamb.

"Who d'you think you're talking to? What d'you think you're at? Having your boy friend round here, leaving his clothes around . . ."

Her anger had settled in the bottom of her mind, smooth and hard.

"Dad. It was a bit warm in the front room. He unfastened his tie. He forgot it. I'm sorry. I'll make sure he gets it back." She reached out for the tie. Dad snatched it back. She went on . . .

"I've not been at anything. If you hadn't insisted on going to the club, I could have been out all evening, anywhere, with anybody and you wouldn't have known. Look, Dad, this is all a lot of mither over nothing. And I'm dead beat and I'd like to get some sleep."

She sat down on the bed as if to pull the bedclothes over her. He lunged a step forward.

"You're not grown up yet, you know. You can't have it all your own way, just because your Mum's not here."

She sprang from the bed.

"Dead right, I don't have it my own way. I have it everybody else's. Kev's got to have his breakfast and tea and his hand held at night, you've got to have your cups of tea, your clean shirt and your nice dinner on Sundays with Gran's lovely apple crumble. You've both got to have a clean house to come home to."

She paused for breath.

"And, on top of that, you want me to pass my exams and be a nice little girl as well."

Suddenly he interrupted her. The words burst out of him.

"That wasn't my idea. That was your Mum's."

"What was?" She was baffled.

"It was your mother's idea you should take your 'O' levels and stop on in the sixth form. I always reckoned you could leave at sixteen if you wanted to. But she had big ideas for you – and herself," he added, almost in a whisper. He raised his voice again.

"So don't think you have to take those exams for my sake. You can leave this summer as far as I'm concerned."

Jan began to say: "Oh, yes, and spend all my time going to the launderette for you and Kev." The words spoke themselves clearly in her mind, but all that came out was "Oh, yes."

He put his hand to his head, as though it hurt.

"Anyway, that's up to you." He spoke calmly as though he'd come upstairs just to talk about her schooling. He moved away on the landing, switching off the light as he went.

"Good night."

"Good night."

He paused on the landing as though remembering something.

"Just watch it, though."

Chapter 11

Dad did not speak again about Peter and in the days that followed he was careful and polite to Jan. There was even a change in tone, as though he were talking to someone his own age. Now and then in the evenings, as they had a cup of tea together, he would talk to her about people on the training course, about small incidents. He seemed to be after her approval for the way he dealt with problems. He spoke to her more as he used to speak to Mum. He said no more about Friday. On that there was a silent agreement. Friday night was his club night and she stopped in to look after Kevin. Peter came round when Kev was in bed and left quietly before Dad came home. Each Friday Dad came home later and Peter stayed longer.

A routine developed. Going into the locker room at school she would find a note in her pocket: "Friday night we come a soul-caking." Or as she sat in the library reference room in the late afternoon there would be a tap on the window and she'd see Pete mouthing the word "Friday".

Soon they did not even bother with words. As soon as Kevin was washed and in bed, she'd pick up the phone, dial Pete's number, let it ring twice (no more in case his mother picked up the receiver) and then ring off. This was his signal to come round. They'd sit in the kitchen over coffee or tea, school books spread out testing one another. Then, often without a word, they'd close the books, go into the front room, make themselves comfortable and, later still, sit watching television like an old married couple. Sometimes he brought cans of beer round with him. Jan removed the cans and other traces of the visit carefully from the room. Pete would clown.

"Kindly hand me my tie. I must not forget that. And my coat, if you please and my shirt, and my . . ."

"Shut your face."

"What is it that marks Jan Whitfield out from the common or garden birds at Gorse Lane Comprehensive? Is it her style, her olde-worlde charm?"

Sometimes she would provide the drinks. One Friday, as she picked up a half-pack of lager from the supermarket, madam remarked, with a pointed glance at the "under 18" notice over the cash desk, "I suppose it's all right, since it is a family order."

To herself, Jan said calmly, "Yes, you old bag. I'm entertaining in my front room tonight, much less draughty than down on the towpath."

To the checkout lady, she said with a false smile, "That's right. We've got company this evening."

Jan took life so easily that she surprised herself. Under her calm there was a bubbling good spirit which showed itself in her conversation and in her answers in class, quick-witted as ever, but now a touch insolent.

She'd get applauding giggles from classmates and some-times a puzzled frown from a teacher. Some days she was in a crazy good humour, entertaining a group of girls, some of whom she'd barely talked to before, with stories. One break, when suddenly heavy rain kept them indoors, she began to tell the story of the sales lady, the supermarket manager and the scene on the tow-path.

In the middle of her telling, she looked about her and saw Sharon and two other former friends eyeing her coldly. Their looks provoked her to go on adding details to the tale, deliberately trying to shock them. As the group around her shrieked with laughter, Sharon turned her back and walked away with her companions. In the quiet after the laughter, Jan heard someone speak at her elbow.

"You know what's up with madam, don't you?"

It was Tina Ellis.

"Eh?"

"She's jealous."

"Green with it."

For all her skittish humour, between Pete and herself there was a quiet intimacy. No big scene by the school gate, clinging on to his arm, slobbering over each other, but discreet signs and glances, just like old lovers.

One night, just before Pete went home, he said to her:

"D'you know what I like about you?"

"What, only like?"

"Give over. What I like is your style."

"My what?"

"You're just – yourself. You don't make a fuss. You

take things or leave them. You're independent. I don't have to worry – is she going to be moody tonight, or will she be round my neck at school, or is she going to start nagging to be taken out?"

"You must have had a lot of trouble with your other girl friends."

"Oh, I don't think of you as a girl friend."

"Oh. What do you think of me as, then?"

"Just Jan. I mean, you'd still be you even if we packed in seeing one another tomorrow."

"Oh." She didn't know what to say about that.

"So that's what I like about you," he said, gave her a deep kiss, took his coat and went.

But such solemn chat was rare. Pete's usual mood was jokey or quietly tender. With him she relaxed. She was herself or that self she would want to be, Jan without care, Jan without problems, Jan without exams, Jan without past, Jan without future, Jan, Jan, Jan and to hell with the rest of the world.

Deeper down within herself, she was aware that if she were contented in a hazy way, Pete's feelings were stronger and more urgent. She knew this and she ignored it, letting his experience and his urgency carry them along, as though they were in a boat and he were rowing, she was drifting, hand trailing in the water, one eye on the passing scene.

They were moving on and she was doing nothing about it, though the inner Jan was aware that the movement was a little faster each time and could not be reversed. But since Mum went she had learnt how not to think about things which disturbed her mood. The point was reached and past before she even realized.

One evening as she dreamed in his arms she found herself, eyes wide, staring into the face of a TV commentator, mouth opening and closing pompously, like a plump goldfish in a bowl. She blew him a raspberry.

At the sound, Pete stirred in her arms.

"Hey, what are you up to?"

Idly she focused her eyes on him, his face six inches away from hers, cheeks flushed, hair damply curled on his forehead. She could see he was offended. His whole appearance reminded her of Kevin, half asleep after his bath on Saturday, protesting about being put to bed. She burst out laughing.

"Eh, lad, am I putting you off your stroke?" she asked.

His mouth pouted and now he looked completely like Kevin in anger. Touched, she took his sweat-damp face on to her breast, stroking his hair as if to get rid of the bad mood. Then she saw in his eyes another mood, an eagerness that touched her even more. Her body relaxed as his grew more tense.

"Jan," he whispered.

"Yes," she answered drowsily.

"Is it all right?"

"If it's not now, it never will be," she heard herself answer, as she drifted away, leaving the other Jan together with Pete.

Later he left the house quietly. Jan had the strange feeling she had taken charge of the two of them. As she watched him go she thought of what Sandra had said.

"Play it their way, take 'em for all you can get."

But Sandra was wrong. They were all like little boys, Dad and all. Taking from them was like stealing sweets from kids.

Next Sunday, the family, for they had started hesitantly to call themselves "the family" again, drove up to Warby.

"My, she does look well. Look at those cheeks. Looking after her Dad and Kev must suit her," said Gran.

"Get off," snorted Granddad. "She's got a feller."

Dad looked away out of the window. Kevin said:

"Hey, she has an' all."

Jan shook her fist at him, then grinned foolishly. But nothing anyone could say could shake her good mood.

Another week came and went, the days floating by. Pete's mood was quieter, there were fewer jokes and she found herself gently poking fun at him, suddenly annoying him, then soothing him calmly, confidently. In one way they seemed closer, yet in another they seemed further apart, as if she were older than him.

In one of his bad moods, she tried to please him by talking of the coming Whitsun and what they might do.

"Let's have some fun before the exams catch up on us, lad."

To her surprise he did not care to talk about it.

"Please yourself. Here, give us a kiss."

At school, her light-hearted mood continued, but she balanced this by working harder than ever. Miss Maudesley looked at her anxiously.

"You try and take it easy over the holiday, Jan. First exam is the Wednesday after we get back, remember."

"Oh, I'll take it easy, like I always do," she answered flippantly.

That Friday, Pete stayed so long that they heard Dad's

car drive up outside and there was an awkward half a dozen word conversation in the doorway, before Pete got away.

On Whit Saturday, Dad announced he would take them all to the seaside, but Jan made an excuse, saying she'd spend the day over her books.

"You lads'll have much more fun without me around."

Dad shrugged. Kev giggled.

"I know what you're up to."

She placed a finger on his snub nose and dented it slightly.

"You think you do, but you don't. See?"

But Kev was right. She hung about the house all day, making a pretence of studying. She got her dinner from the Chinese take away, then took a fancy to do some housework. She cleaned the house from top to bottom, took a load of washing to the launderette and ironed several of Dad's shirts, piling them up demonstratively on his bed. Then she took a long, lazy bath, so full she could hear the overflow running away at the back of the house. As she lay there, letting her long legs float up, she thought about her body. It looked daft to her, but Pete liked it, and Jan was there inside it, so there must be something to her.

She dressed in a new skirt and blouse Mum had bought her just before . . . Then she put on some of the scent Gran had given her at Christmas, slung her bag over her shoulder and walked as casually as she could up to the fairground on the Jubilee Fields. She roved around for an hour making out she was having a marvellous time, waving to some of her class mates who were there with their boy friends, shrieking with laughter and throwing their money about.

When it was almost dark, she found him at last amid his friends at the back of a crowd around the catch-as-catch-can booth. She went up boldly and slipped her arm through his.

He stared at her and blurted:

"What are you after?"

"Give you three guesses," she said impudently.

His mates fell about and punched him. One said, "Come on, gents, he's occupied," and they moved away into the crowd pushing and joking.

For a moment his mood was uncertain, but then he got back his good humour and put his arm around her waist, pressing her to him. They wandered off, she edging him gradually towards the end of the fairground. He let himself be drawn, while she chattered away.

In a dark side street off the fairground she stopped him by a wall and kissed him hungrily.

"Didn't you have any dinner?" His voice was shaky.

"Oh ah. This is for afters. You know me, Dangerous Jan."

She linked arms with him again and they set off down the road, she guiding him steadily towards the river and the towpath. The night air was warm, and the dry ditch below the allotments was full of the scent of spring flowers. In the dark below the bushes, he seemed to hold back from her, but she took his head gently between her hands.

"Come on, lad. I won't say a word – promise."

Chapter 12

When they said good night, at the corner of her street, Pete said casually:

"I think I'll give this Friday a miss, Jan. OK? Exams start the week after and I'm going to put in some heavy work this week."

"But I thought we could work together at our place," she protested. He shook his head.

"Not really. I want to get right into my chemistry. I'll be at it all day and half the night. There'd be no fun just sitting either side of the table, heads in book, would there?"

"Don't know." Jan stuck her lip out.

"Come on," he said, "don't go soft on me. That's not you."

"Oh, all right. Next week, then?"

"Ah, you look out for the next soul-caking announcement."

He kissed her and ran off along the pavement before she could say anything. Jan walked slowly to their house, her happy mood subdued. Well, Pete was right. There'd be plenty of time later. And she could get stuck into some work, as well.

She worked steadily for the rest of the holidays, even through the weekend. And she knew why. She wanted to make the time pass, get back to school and see Pete. She wouldn't try to talk to him. She'd just see him from a distance, just know he was there. And, maybe she'd surprise him, just to show she'd been thinking of him. The thought excited her more and she worked away the last few days before the first exam in a kind of fever, face flushed and eyes smarting. Dad looked at her anxiously, but she sang about the house as though exams were what she'd waited for all her life.

She moved through the first exam day in a dream. Other people swore it was a pig of a paper, but Jan sailed into the questions, the words flowing from her mind on to the paper in an easy stream. She left the exam room early and sat on the school wall in the June sunshine.

Inside the school the pips went, the tannoy squawked. First and second years tumbled out of doors and fought in the yard. From the dining hall came the great noise of scraping chairs and clattering dishes. She wasn't hungry. She waited. She saw him coming past with his mates. As they came closer she sprang from the wall and called his name.

"Pete."

"How did it go?" He sounded wary. She was puzzled.

"Magic. Couldn't have been better," she said. "I was thinking of you when I did the paper. Went like a dream. Must be all that coaching on Friday nights."

He looked around him. She caught his sleeve.

"Listen, Pete. I've got a free afternoon. Let's have a ploughman's at the Red Lion and . . ." she hesitated, "go down the river for a walk, afterwards."

He shrugged.

"I was going for a drink with my mates."

"So? I'll come with you and we can go for a walk afterwards."

"I'm not sure." His face was sullen. She stared.

"Here, what's up, Pete? Have I upset the lad? There, there."

"It's not funny."

"Pete. You are mad at me. But why, what have I done?" She put her face close to his.

"I don't like having things fixed up for me, if you must know."

She jerked back her head.

"Who's fixing things up?"

"You are . . ."

"But, Pete. I just thought it would be fun. Am I not allowed to suggest something?"

He turned his head away.

Jan's voice rose, "You mean it's all right when you start things off, but not when I do it."

He looked round in alarm.

"Hey shut up, will you?"

"What d'you mean?" Her voice hardened. "That's it, is it? Little Jan waits till she's whistled for, does she, eh? Nice little Jan. No trouble little Jan. That's what he likes about her, is it? Turn her on and off like a tap, little Jan."

In the midst of her tirade he walked away blundering through a crowd of fifth year girls who were making big ears round the school gate. Jan made a first step to follow him, then stopped herself and went back towards the school building. In the sky a cloud had come up over the sun and the breeze suddenly felt chill on her arms.

That week there was no note in her coat pocket and on Friday Pete did not come round to the house. For a while she controlled her impatience, then fretfully she took up the phone and dialled his number, let it ring twice and put down the receiver and waited. But no Pete came.

At school on Monday there was no sign of him. There was nothing special in that. Now the exams were in full swing, people were allowed to work at home if they pleased. She told herself that was it. Pete was a demon for work, she knew. He intended to do well. His place at Manchester was waiting for him. He'd get the grades and no messing. She'd just have to wait until he got in touch with her. It was daft, having a row over something like that, just because she'd asked him out. And she had her work, too. Another exam came up. She came to school after a sleepless night and had to struggle to finish her questions. The drive and the elation of the week before had gone.

Another Friday came and no Pete. She sat and waited until waiting gave her a headache that seemed to split her skull apart. She hurried Kevin protestingly early to bed, pushing him up the stairs while he shouted for his Dad. Downstairs again she took the phone, let it ring out in the agreed signal. Pete usually took no more than ten minutes to reach their house. That was six hundred seconds. She waited, then rang again. She waited another ten minutes, and tried once more. This time on the second ring the phone was snatched up at the other end.

Mrs Carey's voice shrilled:

"I don't know who you are but will you stop this stupid ringing and ringing off. You've got the wrong number."

Jan ran up to the bathroom and was sick. Then she undressed miserably and went to bed. To her surprise she went to sleep quickly, slept heavily and awoke next day to find it was midmorning. Dad called her from the kitchen as she came sleepily on to the landing.

"Jan, we're out of coffee."

"Oh, I thought we had loads."

"No, both of those big tins are empty. Can you get some?"

"Hell," she muttered. "No, Dad, I'm right out of cash."

"How come? I thought you had enough money these days."

"Not for that. I had to stock up on flour this week. We were right out."

Mum's little stocks of food and things were giving out one by one.

Dad shouted from the kitchen. "I'm leaving a pound note on the table, Jan. I've got to go out. But we'll have to watch the housekeeping. I'm not made of money, you know."

Jan was in the middle of an angry answer, when the front door slammed.

Another desperate week followed, with two exam papers, one of which was a disaster. She slipped from school quietly after each one, not daring to face Miss Maudesley, recalling her earlier flip remarks. Friday loomed with its promise of a sharper edge to her misery. But her days now were not like those when Mum had first vanished from the house. Then all feeling was numbed – all senses dulled. Now each nerve seemed alive. She felt each moment's unhappiness separately. She knew that she was unhappy and she knew why. This was not an unhappiness that had fallen on her from a clear sky. This was something she had made herself and could not put right. Friday came and went. She sat by herself and did not dare to touch the phone.

On Saturday she had another row with Dad as the housekeeping money ran short again. He grumbled, she snapped. Kevin stared at the two of them and burst into tears. Dad signalled to Jan and the two of them went into the front room and shut the door.

"Listen, Jan love." His voice was quieter now. "I should really have talked to you about this before. I just can't give you any more for housekeeping. We're stuck with it. It was different when I was at Bonner's. I could work over, work weekends and knock up extra. Now I'm on a grant, and I will be until late on next year. After that, OK maybe. But right now, we're strapped. There's the mortgage, rates, light, heating. I've got to put a bit aside for clothes for all of us. Lord knows if we're going to get a holiday this year."

He looked at her pale face.

"I'm sorry to wish this on you while you're taking your exams but we've got to manage somehow. What the housekeeping money won't cover, we can't have."

He stood up, remembering something.

"Hey, Jan. In a drawer upstairs I've got the notebook –" he hesitated, then spoke firmly, "the notebook she used to use to work out the housekeeping. It's got all the items in it. She kept a note of what they all cost, how much we need of each. It's got a little calendar and all in it."

He rushed out and came back a minute later holding the little pocket book. It had a green cover with a small yellow flower in the centre. Jan recognized it instantly, and suddenly felt an unknown qualm of fear as though her spirits had dropped to a new low.

"Thanks, Dad." She turned the book over and unconsciously lifted it to her face. There was a faint trace of Mum's scent.

"Look, love, we're going out to Warby tomorrow. You will come, won't you? Unless you're going out with Pete."

"Oh, no," she said hastily. "That's fine. I'd love to come."

"Right on," said Dad. "Look, I have to go out now. See you teatime."

As Dad pulled the front door to behind him, Jan turned the little notebook over and over, then held it to her face. She opened it at the back, where the calendar fitted into the cover under a transparent plastic sheet. She stared at the dates marked off with a circle round them.

There was a circle early in January, then one at the beginning of February, then no more. None in March, none in April. Mum must have forgotten to mark the date. You could forget to do that if your mind was on other things and the days flew past.

Kevin ran into the front room, shouting.

"Let's be having you. Those who don't want to watch 'Swap Shop' can clear out."

She snapped, "Do you have to make such a bloody row?"

His small face paled. Suddenly she felt ashamed and pushed past him to the door.

Upstairs in her own room, she pulled open the drawer in her dressing-table. Her diary was there under a pile of underwear. She picked it up, dropped it, then took hold of it firmly and flicked open the pages.

She had marked the last date early in May. She counted rapidly. The weeks had slipped away. One, two, three . . . one, two, three, four . . . She was a week – nine days over.

She put the diary away and went downstairs again. That was all right. She'd been two weeks over more than once and a couple of times nearly four weeks had passed before it came. That was all right, then.

But she didn't believe it.

Chapter 13

"That girl's looking peaky again."

Gran looked across the table at Dad. She always did when she talked about Jan. It was an old habit and it made Jan feel about six years old. They'd just finished Sunday dinner at Warby and sat uncomfortably in the heat of the kitchen with the summer sun striking in through the window.

"Ah, she'll be all right after the exams are done, won't you, love?" said Granddad.

Gran's lips puckered.

"I can't see why she bothers."

Dad began to look embarrassed and make signals with his eyebrows at Gran, but she took no notice.

"What good's it going to do now? What they need is a bit more coming in, till our Geoff gets himself set up."

"Ah, they'll manage," said Granddad, looking uncomfortable. "We'll help them, won't we?"

Gran wasn't listening. She had a piece to say and was on the way to say it.

"You can get down, Kev," she snapped. Kev, eyes

round, slipped from the table.

"Shut the back door, love."

Gran half turned to look directly at Granddad.

"She always fancied herself – no, I'm going to say it. Couldn't stay in the works at Cartwright's where she could make a bit extra now and then. Had to go in Personnel, had to go to night school, just when our Geoff's trying to make his way, like a feller should. Always fancy ideas and then what happens."

Jan felt the warmth of anger slowly rise inside her.

"All those exams. It was her idea." Gran ran on.

Whose exams? wondered Jan. Whose idea? It didn't seem to make any difference who Gran was talking about. The words poured out. Granddad looked angry now. Dad looked down at his plate like a boy whose brother is getting a telling off.

Her idea? Jan's mind leapt upon the idea like a cat on a mouse. Dad had said that – it was Mum's idea she should stay on at school and take those exams. Now Gran was saying it. Who was putting whom up to it? Then she pushed the thought away. This was too much to cope with all at once. But still the anger rose. Then she heard her own voice.

"You get a better job if you get your 'O' and 'A' levels."

"That's right," said Granddad. "You need them if you're going to be a teacher or do research and . . ."

"Ah, and the cow starves while the grass grows," responded Gran. "Fancy ideas when what the family needs is a bit in the kitty."

Jan's anger concentrated in a tiny knot of pain above her eyes. She pushed her chair back.

"I'm going out for a walk. I've a headache. I'll see to the dishes when I get back, our Gran."

Outside on the hill road, she heard her name called. Granddad came puffing up behind her.

"Wait on, Jan lass, wait on. I'm winded."

"Sorry, Granddad." He came up alongside her and took her arm. They trudged on up to Borley Top and as she breathed in the warm fragrant air over the moors, Jan felt the pain knot unloosen. They stood at the top and looked out.

"It's a grand view."

She nodded.

"Listen, Jan love. If you need any help, for ought, doesn't matter what it is, you come up here. You shall have it. We hanna much, but . . ."

"Oh, Granddad." The tears stung behind her eyelids, but would not come down. Thoughts shaped in her mind but would not come out. If she could talk to anyone, she could talk to this square little man with his reddish cheeks and blue-scarred chin. But she couldn't talk to anyone, could she? Not him, not Gran, not Dad.

In her bedroom that night, she took out her diary again. You could be three weeks overdue and still be all right. She'd been more than that a year back. It had been terrible, a blanket of pain from head to thigh, and then it had gone, like a bad dream. But then, she hadn't been . . .

She'd thought Pete had been taking care of that. Correction, she hadn't thought. She'd felt things, she hadn't thought. And Pete, did he think she was on the Pill or something? Oh, I like Jan, she looks after herself.

She and Mum had often chatted about these things, but there was a holding back on Mum's part as though she wished Jan didn't have to go through the whole business.

Jan recalled then, as clearly as if she heard the words in that moment, a snatch of conversation overheard as she lay half asleep one night. Mum and Dad came up the stairs, arguing so fiercely they'd forgotten to close their bedroom door.

"It's not safe, there's a heart condition in our family," said Mum, her voice nearly a whisper.

Then Dad, anxiously reassuring, "But they reckon the medical risks are really quite small, less than having a baby, almost . . ."

Then Mum, speaking more loudly:

"Well, I don't like the idea. I'm not going to be on permanent stand-by like an emergency service."

"Sh! Val, you'll wake the kids."

Jan went to sleep finally with the thought: I've been nearly four weeks overdue before. She knew that and held on to what she knew. And that was another fortnight. She could push the problem away for that long and maybe something would happen.

As she shuttled to and fro, home to school, school to library, library to home, she would sometimes have hours pass without thinking about it, without even giving it a name. Now and then it would leap on her from dark ambush. As she walked home along Gorse Lane, she would quicken her pace and run past that overhanging wall, heart beating, skin tight on her skull. She would not slacken her pace until she came to her own turning. Keep the mind clear of that and run and run and get home fast, and tell Mum what had gone wrong and get it all put right.

Ten days passed and nothing happened. One night she was sick before she went to bed: But, that was wrong, wasn't it? Eyestrain, lack of sleep, not enough to eat, it could be anything. She went each day with a feeling of dizziness and nausea not far away. On the way to the shops, she thought of Dr McLeod, ancient white-haired Dr McLeod, smelling of cough drops, giving pats on the head and bottles of jollop. She hadn't been to him for years. Mum kept herself and them away from doctors. Dr McLeod had put those stitches in her leg above the knee when she was thrown off the roundabout on the rec. That was years ago and they stood out white amid the sunburn. They fascinated Pete. He used to trace them with his finger. "Dangerous Jan."

She had seen Pete once or twice since her attempts to phone him. But always from a distance. He was avoiding her and something held her back from going up to him again. Once she had nearly bumped into him near the sixth form block but turned aside when she saw Sharon hanging around chatting brightly.

After that she began to take care to keep out of his way, to be sure he should not think she was begging to be taken back. As her present trouble closed in round her she walked by herself again and did not think of whom she met. As she came from the library in town late one afternoon, she was suddenly face to face with him. He dodged aside and rushed on. She was alone in her own world again, struggling from day to day, swinging between frantic bouts of useless studying, where the words ran from her mind as fast as she read them, and long, empty stretches of time when she sat and stared at nothing.

It could not go on though. At last by an effort of will she determined to do something. In the fourth week, she went to a chemist's on the other side of town and walked up and down outside it, taking her sample bottle out of her handbag, clutching it in her hand, then putting it back again, pretending to look in the window at the toilet display and then finally snapping her handbag shut again and walking away. If I go inside, they'll test the sample and tell me – am I or aren't I. But if I don't go inside they can't tell me that I am, so I can go another few days and maybe something will happen.

Next day she made up her mind to face it again. As she came home she turned into Sandra's front door. She had not seen Sandra for a week. The door was wide open as usual with the sound of the television and Kevin's shrill giggle. Inside, the kitchen was a mess. Dishes crusted with food were piled high on the table. Clothes and underwear were strewn around. Sandra's two sons lounged in the sagging easy chairs. Kevin squatted on the floor, some four feet away from the set. Jan sniffed. Somebody had been smoking in here, but there was no sign of Sandra.

"Where's your Mum?"

The elder of the boys did not even look at her. He jerked his thumb towards the front room.

Jan found Sandra sprawled on the settee. The curtains were closed and the room in near-darkness. She jerked them apart and Sandra moaned. Her face was grey, her lipstick streaked like blood round her mouth. She was drunk.

"Sandra, are you all right?" Jan helped her into a sitting position.

"Bugger off."

"Sandra!"

"Ah, the sod. He just walked out. He just told me to . . . he walked out . . ."

Sandra's voice trailed off.

"Can I get you a cup of coffee, Sandra?"

Jan could not tell if the answer was yes or no. Sandra's head had slipped sideways on the back of the settee.

Jan walked quickly into the kitchen and turned off the television.

"Hey, what was that for?" The elder brother came out of his coma. Jan ignored him. She turned to Kevin.

"You Kevin, go home."

He hesitated.

"Now."

He slouched out of the room and she turned to the others.

"You two, on your feet. Get this place cleaned up. Get those dishes washed up and make your mother a cup of coffee." She drew in a breath, raised her voice and shouted: "Move, before I put my boot up your backside."

She turned for the door. "I'll be back in ten minutes. God help you if it isn't done."

She clumped down the passage, passing Sandra who leaned, bleary-eyed and bewildered, against the door-post.

Chapter 14

Next day Jan made up her mind to talk to Miss Maudesley. There was a slack time before the final exam when those people who had no reason to stick around stayed clear of school, and those who came were busy. The classrooms were half empty and there was more time for a talk which would not be overheard. So on this day Jan screwed herself up to the pitch of thinking about it and talking about it.

She came to school in an excited state, but missed her chance in the morning, for Miss Maudesley was late into school. She hung around hoping to see her, but in the end went into the library and tried to work. Somewhere behind her there was a low murmur of conversation. She could not be sure, but felt rather than heard her own name. She looked round but the talkers were silent. She saw Sharon, who met her gaze insolently as if daring her to ask who was discussing her. Jan turned her back and the whispers began again.

At breaktime in the classroom it seemed the same thing happened yet she could not be sure. Maybe in her upset state she was just hearing things. She wished Miss Maudesley would come. She'd ask to see her after school, have a quiet chat. The pips went and there was no sign of the form tutor. Then, coming from the dining hall at lunch break, Jan saw her going into the classroom, pale-faced and tired. She followed the teacher so quickly she arrived in the room almost on her heels. And too quickly for certain other people.

Near the front of the room, a small group, five or six, broke up as she entered. But Sharon had her back to the door and did not react. Her voice, breathless and high-pitched, ran on even when Jan stood behind her.

"Well, of course she turned him off. First she played hard to get, then she couldn't get enough. She was all over him. It wouldn't be so bad, but she fancies herself – bit like her . . ."

Jan took Sharon by the shoulder.

Her arm, as if it moved on its own, came round and the flat hand cracked against Sharon's face. Jan felt the impact run along her arm, as Sharon fell back against the desk. Then Jan heard her own voice, hard and coarse.

"Come on. Give us one back."

She paused, then raised her arm again. But Sharon burst into wild weeping as another girl put an arm round her. Jan turned for the door, the pleasure of the blow tingling in her shoulder. As she reached the corridor, Miss Maudesley was beside her, then standing in front of her.

"Jan, stop!"

She put a hand on Jan's arm.

"Listen to me. I've tried to talk to you for weeks now. Listen. I know you've had a lot to put up with. But you had no right to do that. Sharon is not to blame for your troubles. You know that. I'll say no more about it, on one condition. That you go in there and apologize to Sharon."

Jan looked past Miss Maudesley's tired face.

"Oh ah. I'll go in and say I'm sorry – that I won't hit her again."

She pushed past and ran down the corridor.

"Jan!"

But she no longer heard. She was running out of the swing doors, over the yard and into Gorse Lane. Now she slowed to a stride and walked and walked as though she could pound her problems into the hard pavement. She did not see where her feet carried her until she was over the railway bridge and in among the tower blocks of the old estate. She turned to the left, ran past the recreation ground, where she'd fallen from the roundabout that day, and gashed her leg.

"Missis, come quick. Jan Whitfield's hurt herself, bad."

Jan's hurt herself bad, so bad she'll never be well again. Poor Jan. Who gives a damn about Jan?

Now she had walked in a wide circle, along a road which doubled back under the railway, towards the other side of town. She was in a shopping centre they rarely used, with bigger shops, department stores where they went to buy big clothes items or for Christmas shopping. Jan looked up. There was Barkways. That was where Mum bought herself a new outfit and a case and drove off to the station with a feller and never came back.

What was she here for? She slowed down. The back

of her legs ached with the strain of her furious walking. Her head pained her now. All the rich, satisfying anger had gone and she felt empty and sick again. She saw a handwritten sign on a tiny cream-painted café front: "Espresso coffee – only the best." She stopped.

In the small, curtained plate glass window was another notice, handwritten too, on a large white card which took up half the window space. She stared. It read:

"Has anyone seen this woman?"

Beneath was a picture of a woman in her forties, dark, pretty and plump in a dress with a big floral pattern. She stood against a sunlit wall, as if by the seaside. She looked shy and motherly.

"Maria Donatelli. Missing from her home since January 23rd, 1980. She is five feet one inch tall, and was wearing a grey suit and cream-coloured shoes. Her family will be deeply grateful to anyone who knows anything about where she is."

Jan felt someone was watching her. She looked up. Through the curtains a plump man in an apron looked at her fiercely. Then he jerked his head away, almost as if telling her to go. She moved off slowly and the man came to the door, looking after her. For a moment she thought he would speak to her, but then he turned and went inside the shop again.

She walked farther along the pavement until she came to an off-licence.

It was nearly closing time and the man inside was beginning to pull the blinds down on his window display. Seeing him made up Jan's mind, or brought something to the front of her mind which had been lurking there for days.

She went inside and shortly afterwards came out carrying a bottle wrapped in brown paper. It had cost the rest of the shopping money.

Breathing faster, she crammed the packet into her bag and set off for home.

Chapter 15

Kevin was waiting for her when she arrived home. The neighbour's front door was shut and the noise of their television reached her only faintly through the passage wall. Jan said nothing to Kev but quietly made his tea and packed him off into the front room. She carried her bag up to her room, unwrapped the gin bottle she had bought and put it on the floor of her wardrobe. Did she have to drink all that to make any difference? Would she be able to? She'd tasted it once, scented and powerful. It made her feel sick. Still, she wasn't going to try it tonight. She'd have to wait till Friday, when Dad went out.

But there was no waiting. Her father came home early, his face serious. He wasted no time.

"Jan, I've got to go out again almost right away. There's a meeting about the course, then some of the students are getting together afterwards – end of term."

He waited, she said nothing.

"Jan, listen. I had a phone call from school. I'm not sure if I want to know what you've been up to."

Jan shrugged. He tried to make a joke of it.

"First Kev, then you. They want me to go in to discuss your future at the school."

"Well, if they don't want me back, you'll be well suited, won't you?"

He started to answer, then stopped. Instead he took a deep breath, as if counting to ten.

"I'm not arguing the toss about that. We'll talk at the weekend. Things have got in a mess. They need sorting out. But not now, or we shall fall out."

He took his cup of tea and walked upstairs to his room. Jan tried to eat her tea, but the bread tasted like cardboard.

While Dad got ready to go out, Jan sat in the front room with Kevin, watching the box. He was wary of her, a little awed at the way she had kicked the two tearaways next door around. She forced herself to smile at him. She didn't want any mither with him this evening. She wanted time to herself. But it was no good pushing him. She didn't want him moaning to Dad when he came home. Little Kev was getting the measure of his Dad and his sister and he wasn't above playing them off against one another as he used to play off Mum against Dad. For a second she hated the little tyke, then told herself not to be stupid. He was seven years old and only a kid.

The door slammed, the car started outside. Dad was off for the evening. One down, one to go, she thought. She was getting light-headed. No breakfast, hardly any lunch, hardly any tea. She dragged herself back into the kitchen and boiled an egg, made some toast. Toasted, the bread was just edible. Kevin ambled after her and she boiled him an egg, too. Finding her in a more friendly mood he started to chatter. Controlling her growing impatience, she answered him now and then, just as Mum used to do, letting the stream of words flow on.

"You're not listening, Jan."

"Getaway. Course I am. I heard every word."

"Well, what did I just say?"

"You're not listening, Jan," she mimicked his voice.

"You're a pig."

"You're a pig's brother. Go and watch 'Star Trek'."

She looked at the clock and wondered how she could make the hands turn faster. She was going to do something about it tonight. Something crazy. But better than doing nothing.

The television sounded again from the front room. She heard Kev shriek with laughter. "Star Trek"? What did it matter what he watched? It was ridiculous. Everything she did in this house was just as Mum used to do it. She was a prisoner to that routine. She did things as though they were the only thing to do.

But she did not know why she did them. Did Mum know? She seemed to, but how could you tell? She'd taken Mum's place and she didn't even know who Mum was. And that funny little café owner with his notice – if you find my wife please let me know. He must want her back badly. There was her Dad going about it quietly, hoping, believing that people might never find out. But Mr Donatelli didn't care who knew. His wife had gone away and he wanted her to come back, and as long as she did, what did he care if the whole world knew? Suddenly Jan thought she'd like to go back to that café and talk to him.

Time had passed. She called for Kev and he came quietly. They messed about a bit in the bathroom, splashing one another. When he was in his pyjamas, ready for bed, she remembered.

"Now, listen, Kev. I'm going to have a nice long bath. So if you want the toilet, you go now before you go to bed."

"Suppose I want to later on?"

"Then you can tie a knot in it."

He giggled and thumbed his nose at her. She chased him out of the bathroom and round his bedroom till his giggles changed to hiccups. She wrestled him into bed and tucked him in.

"It's still light."

"Course it is. It's summertime. I'll close the curtains."

"Jan, will we go away this summer holiday?"

"How d'you mean?"

"I mean we haven't any money, not with Mum being away."

"Ah, get off with your bother. We'll think of something. Come on, Kev, off to sleep."

At last he was quiet. She waited fifteen minutes to be sure and then began to run the bath, a thin stream of water to make it hotter. While she stripped off her clothes the steam filled the bathroom and clouded the windows. She drew the plastic curtains. Not that anyone could see through, but she wanted to close herself in. She started to close the bathroom door, then remembered the gin bottle. Naked she padded along the landing.

"Jan," Kev called from the bedroom.

"What is it?"

"Can I use the bathroom?"

"Hell!" She grabbed her dressing-gown.

"Come on and make it quick."

He ran in, leaving the door open.

"Hey, is this a Turkish bath?"

"No, I'm going to boil myself. Hurry up."

"OK, OK." He ran as she flapped her hand at his rear. Another wait now, until he settled down again in bed. A sudden splashing outside told her the bathroom overflow was working. She rushed in and switched off the hot tap. Then without thinking she plunged in her hand to lift the plug. The pain was unbearable. She swore and jerked back her hand. A red patch ran up her arm to the elbow. She gritted her teeth, padded out to the kitchen and picked up a big saucepan. Carefully she ladled out water from the top of the bath until the level was lowered. Now what?

She picked up her clothes and carried them into her bedroom, throwing them on to her bed. Now back into the bathroom, take off her dressing-gown, hang it up and lock the door. She sat down on the toilet top and picked up the bottle and a glass from the bathroom cabinet. Had little Square Eyes seen the bottle, she wondered. Well, what did it matter?

Did you drink it before you got in or while you were in? She poured a glass and drank, it went down the wrong way and threw her into a fit of coughing. It was like scented medicine. She drank more. It was a little better the second time and still better the third. The steam in the bathroom and the gin fumes in her nostrils made her feel dizzy. She stood up, hauling on the pipe above the toilet. Pouring another glass, she set it down on the floor. Then she hoisted one foot over the rim of the bath. For a second she thought her skin was coming off. Sidling along to ease the pain she slipped. Her free foot knocked over the glass and the other leg plunged into the steaming water. In desperation, as the shock wave of blistering pain ran through her skin, she pushed against the bathroom wall and clawed out wildly in the other direction. Her leg came clear of the bath and one arm connected with the washbowl. Sliding sideways, she struck her hip on the edge of the bath. But now she was free of that torturing water.

She stood naked and dripping, her leg mottled with angry red patches. Surely the skin must peel off. The pain from her hip forced itself on her attention. She sat down once more on the toilet top and picked up the glass. Filling it again she began to drink, more quickly. Now it seemed to go down smoothly. The pain and the smarting became less and her thoughts began to grow more pleasantly, dreamily confused.

If she could try again, it wouldn't hurt so much, perhaps. If she could only get right into the water.

She had one foot on the edge of the bath when the door handle rattled.

"Jan, I want to use the toilet."

"Go to bed," she yelled.

"Can't wait," he answered and began to thump on the door.

She started forward, slipped on the wet floor and her flailing arms struck the bathroom cabinet. The glass shelf beneath it came down and shattered into the wash bowl.

"Sod the flaming thing to hell," she screamed.

"Wait till I tell your Dad what you said," called Kevin

outside the door. In two strides she had it open and while he stared open-mouthed at her nakedness, she struck him two swinging blows to either side of the head.

"Now will you get to bed?"

He fell back in front of her, howling with pain and fear. Still naked, she pursued him into the bedroom and, seizing him from behind, flung him into the bed, covered him up and stalked out. His wails and sobs sounded behind her, but she ignored them.

But back in the bathroom the last lingering intention to get into the water had vanished. Her anger slowly gave way to a muzzy indifference to everything. She yanked out the plug and let the water slide away. She opened the window to release the steam, swept up the broken glass into the dustpan and mopped up the water on the floor. The bottle, miraculously, was still intact and half full. She picked it up, snatched her dressing-gown from the floor and walked hazily downstairs.

At half past eleven, her father came home to find his son awake and roaring with now forced tears, and his daughter lying on the settee, hair over her face and an empty gin bottle lying on the carpet beside her.

She opened her eyes as he came in.

"What's this, Jan? Kevin tells me you . . ."

She rolled off the settee and crouched on the floor. Her voice was slow and a little slurred. But he was not listening.

"Jan, it doesn't matter how you feel about life, about – your Mum not being here. You have no right to take it out of little Kev. He's got enough to put up with."

"Oh, yes?" She squinted up at him from a foot above the carpet.

"Yes, Jan. It's hard for you. But you've just got to face up to your responsibilities."

She winched herself up to her knees.

"What responsibilities?" Her voice slowly became clear and precise.

"To the rest of the family. You can't live for yourself all the time."

Pressing down with her heels, she launched herself upwards. Now she was standing, but swayed to and fro. She brushed past him and walked to the door. She stood, one hand on the door frame, gathering her unfastened dressing-gown about her.

"Shall I tell you what I think about the rest of this family? I'm sick of the rest of this family. I'm sick of you and I'm sick of Kev. I'm sick of the food you eat and your dirty plates and your dirty underwear in the washing. That's what I'm living for and it's so marvellous I'm going to forget my exams and spend all my time doing it."

Now the words lurking in the depth of her mind surfaced in a great boiling rush.

"I couldn't understand before about Mum. I think I hated her at first, but I didn't dare think about it. But now I think I know why she jacked it in. I think I know why she walked out. The only thing that amazes me is why she waited so bloody long . . ."

There was more to say, but his hand across the side of her face cut it short. She felt no pain. Her eyes were fixed upon the expression of shock on his features as he saw what he had done.

Then she swung round and ran up the stairs, a great feeling of relief welling up inside her. She was going to cry. She was going to cry for the first time since she was twelve. And once safe in her bedroom, lying across her bed in the dark, she felt the tears explode from her and rain down, as her chest heaved in deep moaning sobs.

When she was wept out she went to sleep. She dreamt she floated through the sky on an enormous balloon that swayed and bobbed and carried her along, and swelled and swelled until it swallowed her, until she was the balloon and grew and grew and grew.

She was awake, awake in the grey dawn light and leaping to her feet, throwing the bedclothes aside. It had come. Her period had come after all. She rushed into the toilet.

Five minutes later, she heard Dad's sleepy voice from his bedroom.

"Jan. Why are you singing in the bathroom at five o'clock in the morning?"

She tiptoed back into the bedroom and lay down on the bed. Her relief was the sweetest feeling she had ever known.

Lying half-awake on top of the bedcover, she began to think hazily about what she would do tomorrow. First she'd have a sort out with Dad. Then she'd see about what to do after that. She'd stop living from day to day and start planning.

Slowly she drifted off to sleep and began to dream of Mum coming home again.

Chapter 16

The picture of Mum was still fresh in Jan's mind when she awoke. Only as she struggled out of bed did it fade. She went downstairs to find the house empty. She'd overslept. Dad and Kev had gone and she was late for school. But she felt calm and moved deliberately about the kitchen, ate breakfast and then walked slowly to school to arrive just in time for her final exam.

No one spoke to her, no one looked at her. She returned the compliment, enjoying her own company. Clear headed she answered her questions swiftly and confidently. She'd done well, she knew. If she'd taken every paper in this way there'd be no doubt she would have top grades. Bit late in the day, but not to be helped. Before noon she had handed in her papers and got clear of the school, picking up a few odds and ends from her locker and stuffing them into her bag as she went. Five minutes later she was on the familiar Gorse Lane trail leading to home, and not once looking back. But she wasn't going home just yet. She had a plan, an idea which had come into her mind, early that morning.

As she walked along she whistled and now she came to think of it she did whistle rather well. A blackbird on a tree in one of the gardens sang out at her as she passed and she answered him (was it a him?) with a long trill which made a woman bending down to poke at her flower bed, start and look up.

"Did you do that, love?"

"I did an' all."

At Cartwright's main gate she turned in without halting her pace. She knew that every Friday in summer they interviewed school leavers for jobs.

They called it "interviewing", but Jan knew from her mother that it was just name, address, age, exams and how's your father. If they had room for you in that big glass football pitch they called a production department, you were in and the nuts and bolts awaited you for the rest of your life. She didn't fancy spending her life working in Cartwright's. But what she intended to do between now and the next school year was to earn some cash money. With that up her jumper she could sort things out properly with Dad. What was it Sandra said? "The men have it their way because they pay their way." There was some truth in that. She'd learnt a bit these past few months, had Jan. But there was more to it than that. For all this talk about taking Mum's place, she was still being treated like a kid. And she thought, wryly, sometimes she felt like a kid.

Well, she could start by earning her living for a bit, get the school out of her hair. With this she marched in through the swing doors of the office block at Cartwright's. She knew the way, down a long passage and into a waiting room outside the Personnel Office, where

Mum had worked. She could see through a glass door panel a man in a light grey suit sitting at a desk and beyond him a couple of girls at typewriters. She turned to find somewhere to sit down, and stopped.

The waiting room was full. All the seats were taken and they'd brought in a load of steel chairs from the canteen. There must have been fifty girls there and they all stared at her. A good half of them were from Gorse Lane, some of them she knew. There were no chairs left and she found a space of wall to lean on. After a while a girl came from the inner office and took her name, age and other details. Then she called two people from the other side of the room and the three went through the doorway. Conversations started again.

Someone nudged her. She turned to see Tina Ellis perched at the end of a bench further along the wall.

"Hey, come and sit down."

Jan hesitated and one of the other girls on the bench said:

"We're in order here."

"Bully for you," said Tina. "Now give over and budge up a bit."

Reluctantly the girls made room and Jan sat awkwardly on the edge of the bench.

"Hey," said Tina Ellis in her ear. "You're not after a job, are you?"

"Well, I'm not here for the beer."

"Thought you were going in the sixth form."

"Well, right now, I need a job."

"I've got to have one," went on Tina. "There's five of us and our Dad reckons we can't manage any more on what he knocks up – and he's working all the hours God sends."

Jan took a quick look at Tina's face, suspecting there might be a dig at her in those remarks. Then she thought – so what, we need the money. Tina was rattling on.

"Mind you, I reckon we're wasting our time. My aunt lives next to a girl in Personnel. She said they had thirty vacancies. I came down early and there was all this mob."

"Why can't they take the first thirty and have done, then?" asked Jan.

Tina shrugged: "I suppose they reckon they can pick and choose now, so they're making the most of it."

Ah, said Jan to herself. We didn't think of that, did we? Go and get a job at Cartwright's, they'll take any idiot who wants to knock up a bit for the Costa del Sol next year. So, why shouldn't they take an idiot like Jan who's suddenly found she needs money.

She dug in her bag and got out a text book and settled down to read it. There was no point, but it passed the time. Some of it was even interesting when you weren't obliged to stuff it into your head. She took a side glance at Tina as if to excuse herself for not talking. That was funny. A few weeks ago she wouldn't have been seen dead talking to Tina Ellis. But Tina was busy talking to a girl on the other side. Time passed, more people went in to Personnel and the crowd in the room dwindled.

"I'm starving. Think it's worth hanging on?"

Jan realized she was being spoken to. She looked up. Tina was still there. The others had gone.

"Might as well."

Tina made a face, then nodded, as though they'd just agreed on something. Both sat in silence for a while, then:

"Tina Ellis!"

The girl from Personnel was calling from the open door.

Tina got up, then turned to Jan.

"Hey, wait on for us, will you?"

Embarrassed, Jan nodded. A few moments later her name was called and she went into the Personnel Office. At one side sat the man she had spotted earlier through the glass door, fair haired and smart in his striped shirt and broad tie, talking across his desk to Tina Ellis.

"Janice Whitfield?"

A neatly-dressed woman, black hair flecked with grey, who sat at another desk to the right, out of sight of the doorway, called her and pointed to a chair.

As she spoke, the man turned his head in her direction and she saw he was young, perhaps eight or ten years older than herself.

"Sit down, Janice, please." The woman smiled at her.

"Do you really want a job in production?"

Jan stared. The woman went on.

"I should have thought someone taking as many 'O' levels as you are would be going on to college."

The words offended Jan, though she could not make out why. She wanted to say something sharp, but that would be stupid. Instead she said cautiously:

"I was just thinking about a job for the holidays for a start."

There was a slow shake of the head.

"The way things are, these jobs are going first to people who want to stay."

"I didn't realize. Well . . ." She half got up to go but the woman raised her hand.

"If you were interested in an office job, and I'd have thought that was more in your line, and if you were interested in staying, we might find something for you." She went on quickly. "You'd get day release and you could go to college."

Jan frowned. She hadn't bargained for this.

"As a matter of fact, we need someone in Personnel, don't we, Mr Thompson?"

Jan was on her feet now. She could not be sure but she felt that the young man had made some kind of signal to the woman at the desk. She looked surprised, then quickly recovered, smiled at Jan and said:

"Anyway, let us know if you are interested, Janice."

Jan mumbled "yes" and went quickly into the outer office. So they needed someone in Personnel did they – as if she didn't know. But what was that young man on about, signalling to the woman?

The outer room was empty now. The interviews were over and everyone had gone for their lunch. What should she do? Go home? The idea of the empty house did not attract her.

Outside in the works yard, the warmth of the sun caught her by surprise. It seemed ages since she'd been out in the fresh air. Maybe she'd go for a walk.

"Oh, there you are."

In front of her, dawdling along, was Tina Ellis.

"I thought you'd gone, you were in there so long. What were you on about?" asked Tina.

Jan shrugged. She didn't know that she wanted to talk about it to Tina or anyone else just now. But Tina didn't seem to notice.

"I'm starving. Are you going in the Red Lion? I expect the other lot will have finished and gone by now," she said.

Why not? Jan fell into step beside Tina as they crossed Gorse Lane, heading down a side street towards the pub. Leading the way, Tina paused a second inside the saloon swing door, then nodded to the right. Over her shoulder Jan saw, in one corner, a group of sixth formers, Pete among them. She overtook Tina and headed for the opposite corner finding a seat which put her out of sight behind a pillar. Lunchtime was nearly over and there was little left but cheese and rolls. Tina ate rapidly.

"Didn't have any breakfast. I can't stand making it. Dad always wants his egg and bacon. The smell of fat in the morning turns me up. Don't know how our Mum put up with it so long."

She chattered on. Jan felt she was being drawn into talking about their family.

She was unwilling, yet why should she keep quiet? Why should she think she was any different from other folk – they were in the same boat, weren't they? She still remembered Tina's accusation in the schoolyard – "snob". Was that what they were, trying to "get on", buying that crummy little house, taking exams, climbing up, being knocked down again?

Through her thoughts she heard Tina's voice.

"I hated our Mum at first. I felt sorry for our Dad. I'm not so bloody sure these days. Trouble is there's our Gary and the twins. They've got to be looked after. If it wasn't for them, I'd take off myself."

"What would you do?"

Suddenly Tina wasn't listening. She nudged Jan, cocking her head to one side. Pete was at the bar. She could look at his face in profile. Either he hadn't noticed her or he was still ignoring her. So what, she told herself. But it still hurt.

"Big head," said Tina. She didn't care how loud she spoke.

"Eh?"

"It's all done on purpose, you know. He came up this end of the bar so you could have a good look at him."

"Give over," said Jan.

Tina snorted.

"Well, they're all big heads, aren't they? Think they're the answer to a maiden's prayer."

Jan grinned reluctantly at that. Now they were on safe ground, talking about "them". Tina was giving her a pep talk, boosting her morale. Did she need it, she asked herself? Yes, she did. The hurt was still there. Only her pride was stronger. Her pride was the strongest thing she had. It made her do all kinds of stupid things but it was the most certain thing she knew.

"They're all the same, anyhow. Love you and leave you, my aunt says. Hey, Jan, want another? I'll get 'em."

"Just a tonic."

"Keep the weight down, eh. Wish I had your figure,

Jan. I just have to look at food and I get fat."

Tina sat down again. Pete had gone back to his corner.

"Hey, there's a girl round our way, been having it off with the insurance man." Tina nudged Jan. "She's got one in the oven now and he's stopped calling. Lost her no-claim bonus."

Tina chuckled. Jan was listening closely now.

"Do you know what the silly cow did?"

Jan shook her head.

"She went out and bought a bottle of gin and made herself a hot bath. But she couldn't make her mind up, so she drank it all first, then tried to get in the bath afterwards, fell over and cut her head open. They had to take her to Casualty. Things people do."

"She must have been desperate," said Jan.

"Desperate? I'd have to be desperate to try that old rubbish. Bloody gin bath. They used to believe that in our gran's day. Better safe than sorry, I reckon. Why didn't she go round to the clinic in the first place? Why didn't our Mum go there, come to that, instead of having four of us?"

She paused and shook her head.

"Course, if she'd done that, maybe I wouldn't have been here, would I? Makes you think."

Tina nudged Jan again.

"Now there's a touch of class for a change. More my type, the older man."

Jan looked round. At the bar was the young man in the grey suit from Cartwright's Personnel Department.

"He interviewed me, you know. Said he wasn't sure

whether he could take me on. I nearly said I'd take him on any time."

Jan barely heard what Tina said. Something else had come into her mind. The young man was speaking to the landlord. The sound of his voice, an unusual accent for this part of the world, somewhere from the south, caught her attention, stirred a memory, a hurtful one.

It had been his voice on the phone, that Monday. He had hesitated before telling her Mum hadn't come into work – as though he were hiding something.

Chapter 17

"I suppose you're off fellers just now."

Tina was still talking. Jan grinned at her to show she
was listening, but her mind was busy elsewhere. That
Mr Thompson had recognized her in the office. He knew
it was her mother who had worked in Personnel. Only
the woman who'd interviewed her didn't know. That
was why he signalled to her to stop talking about a job in
Personnel. He hadn't wanted Jan to be upset. That was
nice. Or maybe he just didn't want another Whitfield in
the office – unreliable. No, there was more to it than that,
she felt sure. That young man knew something about
Mum. She felt a sudden excitement.

Now Tina was getting up, snapping her handbag
shut.

"Jan, I've got to go. I'm picking the twins up from the
minder early today. See you around, eh?"

"OK, Tina. Hope you get a job."

"Thanks, love. Same to you." Jan watched her push
through the swing doors across the bar. Life was funny.
Here she was chumming up with Tina Ellis, the last

person in the school . . . Well, she reflected, they had more in common than a good many others. Not just likes and dislikes, but real things. So much had changed in the last few months. She, Jan, had changed.

And right now, she thought, she was going to do something she would never have dreamed of doing before.

She stood up and walked round the bar to the far end of the saloon, to the table where the young man from Cartwright's sat. He was alone, his glass almost empty. She stood by the table and he looked up, surprised.

"Can I have a word with you, Mr Thompson?"

He frowned.

"If it's about a job, then you'd better come and see us in the office."

"No, it's not, it's more – personal."

He looked round quickly. The saloon had almost emptied now. Even Pete and his mates had gone. She hadn't even noticed that.

"Sit down," he said, still looking embarrassed. She sat and placed her hands on the edge of the table as if to steady herself.

"I'm Janice Whitfield. My mother . . ."

He nodded.

"I know. I recognized you."

"You what?" Jan's hand was too slow to stop the words bursting out.

"Your mother always had a picture on her desk of your father and you, and your little brother. What was he called . . . ?"

"Kevin."

"That's it." He leant forward, speaking quietly.

"Look, I'm sorry about what happened in the interview. Miss Hardwick's new in Personnel. She didn't know about . . . I was trying to tell her . . ."

"How do you mean?"

"Well, I thought it might be unpleasant for you to have it mentioned – I mean, as good as offering you the job your mother . . ."

He hesitated.

"My mother walked out on, you mean?"

"It hasn't . . . I mean, she hasn't . . . We haven't filled the vacancy." He looked around again.

"Look, Miss Whitfield. If I tell you something, will you keep it quiet?"

"Listen, Mr Thompson. I'm not being funny, but our family keeps secrets like nobody's business. That's one thing we do well."

He pursed his lips at the bitter sound of her voice.

"Your mother is missed in the office. She was – special."

He paused a second, finished his drink and put down the glass. Then he began to speak again eagerly, as though this were something he had waited to tell someone.

"I'd just started in the department when she moved into the office from production. It was all being reorganized. She was supposed to be on general office duties, but what she did was put everything in order – files, appointments, registers, everything. She was a natural, you know. I mean, most women are neat and know where to put things, but she thought ahead. She acted as though she were running the office. I could see she was worth her weight in gold."

He spoke with pride, like a small boy.

"I was the one who suggested she go to evening classes, get herself some qualifications. They were getting office manager's work out of her for little more than typist's pay. She didn't like to at first. Women always need pushing . . . and I got the feeling it was getting heavy at home."

He took a deep breath and looked at her closely. Jan said nothing, afraid that he might decide to stop talking. But he went on, speaking awkwardly.

"We were friends. I know that sounds stupid, but it's true. I thought a lot of V- your Mum. She was smart, I mean she looked after herself.

"She didn't yak all the time like some. She talked sense. She talked a lot about you. She was proud of you. She was sure you would go on to college. She was proud of your Dad, too. She admired the way he was ready to take a cut in pay, go back to school . . ."

He stopped again, as though afraid he was getting carried away. The silence embarrassed them both. Jan noticed that her knuckles, where she held the edge of the table, were white. She relaxed her grip and rubbed her fingers together.

"Mr Thompson. There's something I must ask you about my Mum – going."

He frowned as though unsure what she might say.

"I spoke to you on the phone. It was the first night." He nodded.

"You said she hadn't been into work. That wasn't true, was it?"

"It was," he insisted, but his eyes did not meet hers.

"Hell," he said. "Look – Jan. It was true in one way, not in another. Your mother didn't come in that day, but I had seen her."

"You did?"

He looked round in alarm. But there was no one close enough in the bar to hear her.

"She made me promise to keep quiet. There was something she couldn't tell me. She'd been upset about something for weeks. Her work was suffering, but she couldn't bring it out. She was trying to keep under control. She wouldn't discuss it. I got the feeling there was no one she could talk to. If Miss Hardwick had been with us, it might have been easier. But old Foxleigh, you couldn't discuss anything with him. The girls in Personnel were too young. And I – well, we used to talk about a lot of things. I'd have done anything to help her, but this was something she couldn't discuss with anyone."

"Anyone?"

He shrugged. "I'm sorry, Jan. I'm not used to this sort of thing. We get all kinds of problems in Personnel. But I've never seen one from the inside. Your mother. She just felt she had to go. Why, or where, I just don't know. She asked me to help her. I took half an hour off from work. No one else knew. She asked me to drive her to the station."

The young feller.

Jan whispered. "It was you."

He looked puzzled.

"The inquiry agent told Dad she was seen at the station with a young man. We thought . . ."

"You thought . . . no, that was me. I was just giving

her a hand. I couldn't say no, could I?" ·

Jan shook her head slowly. Then suddenly:

"Where did she go, Mr Thompson? Which train?"

"I don't know, honestly. She said goodbye at the entrance. I never even saw which platform. She just said thank you, shook hands, took her case and went."

He brushed at the lapels of his jacket.

"I couldn't know . . ."

"Mr Thompson," said Jan. "She didn't leave word . . . she just went . . . and we thought . . ."

Now he shook his head again, vigorously, his eyes hurt.

"No. I don't understand. I just helped her. She was – a friend."

He stopped as though remembering something.

"That inquiry agent was at the office, poking around. There was nothing I could tell him. She cleared out her desk. Everything personal was gone.

"She had this picture of the rest of you which I told you about. The Friday before, she wrapped it up, put it in her bag and took it with her. I'm sure of that."

Chapter 18

Jan got clumsily to her feet, the stool falling behind her. Her eyes filled with tears.

"Are you all right?" The young man was standing, too.

She turned for the door. He followed her. Outside in the afternoon sun, she groped in her bag for a handkerchief and pressed it to her eyes. She bit her lips hard and swallowed. He was standing behind her, asking again if she was all right. She answered but could not look at him.

"Yes, thank you."

He came closer.

"I'm sorry. I didn't want to upset you."

Now she could face him.

"It's not your fault, Mr Thompson. And you haven't upset me. It's just . . ."

"Just what?" He was baffled.

"It's just I'd got used to – things. And now, it's different."

"Different?"

He touched her elbow. They began to walk along the road, towards Cartwright's.

"I can't explain. It's just different."

"Is it worse?"

She shook her head. "No . . . no, it's not worse. It's just . . . I've got to start again."

"I'm sorry, I don't understand."

"I don't really understand myself."

They had reached the corner by the works gate. She turned to him.

"Thanks for talking to me. You've helped me no end."

"Helped?"

"Oh, yes."

"I wish I really had."

He held out his hand.

"If you truly want a job at Cartwright's, anywhere, I'll do my best to help you whatever you'd like to do."

"Thank you."

She drew her hand from his.

"Get in touch," he said. "You know the number."

She nodded. As he turned to go he spoke, as though against his own will.

"I didn't expect . . ."

"Didn't expect?"

"You'd be so like your mother."

Then he had gone inside the gate and she was alone in the afternoon sun. She began to walk away, slowly, head bent to the ground, not watching where she went, her mind going over each word of the conversation. She heard a train go by beneath her feet and knew she had crossed the railway line and was walking through the old estate, that way she had gone before on the day she'd fought with Sharon and run out of school. She'd gone running back to the place where they'd lived before, to the rec ground where she'd played, trying to get back into the past, where Mum could put everything right.

But who could put things right for Mum, when she ran away? No one to talk to, not Dad, not even her own parents. Mum was a voluntary orphan, wasn't she? And not even Granddad at Warby could help, because Gran there didn't like Mum. Jan knew suddenly that Warby Gran was jealous of Mum. All she ever thought of was Dad, her son.

Mum was on her own all the time, and Jan hadn't understood. Clever Jan, who knew so much, couldn't even see when her own Mum was miserable.

She stopped in the rec ground and sat down on one of the seats. Women were out in the sunshine, with toddlers and pushchairs, helping them in and out of the swings, on and off the slides, picking them up, brushing them down, wiping noses, kissing them better. It went on all through their lives. But who picked you up and brushed you down when you had your own kids?

In the afternoon sunlight, into Jan's toiling mind, came a picture, clear and harsh, of Gorse Lane, the estate, the bridge, Cartwright's, the junior school, the senior school, the old people's home. She saw the women going to and fro each day and with them the girls, first in push-chairs, then hand in hand, then on their own: school, Cartwright's, home, on and on, like the film loops they used in school, round and round, round and round.

With a wrench she pulled her mind from it, got to her feet and marched away from the rec, through the alley into the shopping centre. Break away, run, escape.

But what should she, Jan, do? There was Dad and Kev. Dad had been struggling in his own way, taking exams, trying to be somebody. But it was all him, wasn't it? He was still Gran's bright boy, doing well. Look after him, Jan, and little Kev, too.

There had to be another way. Where could you run to? But you couldn't just put up with things. She wasn't made that way. She stopped in her stride. She was in the shopping centre now, near the off-licence where she'd bought the gin bottle and hurried home, that day, years ago. Yet it was only yesterday. Then the row with Dad. She hadn't spoken to him since.

So much had happened in that time. She'd finished her exams. She'd been offered a job; she'd a choice to make. She'd met Mr Thompson.

And he'd told her about Mum, Mum going away. Mum wrapping her family photo in tissue paper, putting it in a safe place, and taking the train to nowhere. Not a word to anyone.

Now she was in front of that little café – Donatelli's. The blinds were down. It must be early closing. But the notice and the picture of Mrs Donatelli were gone from the window.

What had happened? Had she come back? Or had he given up? He hadn't cared what the world thought. He didn't go secretly and quietly so that other people shouldn't know. What mattered to him was seeing his wife again.

What mattered to Dad? Or to Kev? Or to Jan? Was it what happened to them, or what happened to Mum? What sort of a choice did Mum have?

Jan turned on the pavement and began to walk back the way she had come. She was clear in her mind now about what she wanted to do, about work, earning money, about studies. She was going home to talk to Dad, to talk to him about all these things, but most of all about Mum. There had to be an end to silence.

What had happened to Mum was what really mattered. Because that had everything to do with what was going to happen to Jan.

Some more titles in Lions Teen Tracks:

☐ **Tell Me If the Lovers are Losers** *Cynthia Voigt* £2.25
☐ **In Summer Light** *Zibby Oneal* £1.95
☐ **Happy Endings** *Adèle Geras* £2.25
☐ **Strictly for Laughs** *Ellen Conford* £1.95
☐ **The Warriors of Taan** *Louise Lawrence* £2.25
☐ **Second Star to the Right** *Deborah Hautzig* £1.95

All these books are available at your local bookshop or newsagent, or to order direct from the publishers, just tick the titles you want and fill in the form below.

NAME (Block letters) _____

ADDRESS _____

_____

Send to: Collins Childrens Cash Sales, PO Box 11, Falmouth, Cornwall, TR10 9EP

I enclose a cheque or postal order or debit my Visa/Mastercard to the value of the cover price plus:

UK: 60p for the first book, 25p for the second book, plus 15p per copy for each additional book ordered to a maximum charge of £1.90.

BFPO: 60p for the first book, 25p for the second book plus 15p per copy for the next 7 books, thereafter 9p per book

Overseas and Eire: £1.25 for the first book, 75p for the second book, thereafter 28p per book.

Credit card no: _____

Expiry Date: _____

Signature: _____

Lions reserve the right to show new retail prices on covers which may differ from those previously advertised in the text or elsewhere.

Some more titles in Lions Teen Tracks:

☐ **Come a Stranger** *Cynthia Voigt* £2.25
☐ **Waiting for the Sky to Fall** *Jacqueline Wilson* £1.95
☐ **A Formal Feeling** *Zibby Oneal* £1.95
☐ **If This is Love, I'll Take Spaghetti** *Ellen Conford* £1.95
☐ **Moonwind** *Louise Lawrence* £1.95

All these books are available at your local bookshop or newsagent, or to order direct from the publishers, just tick the titles you want and fill in the form below.

NAME (Block letters) _____

ADDRESS _____

_____

Send to: Collins Childrens Cash Sales, PO Box 11, Falmouth, Cornwall, TR10 9EP

I enclose a cheque or postal order or debit my Visa/Mastercard to the value of the cover price plus:

UK: 60p for the first book, 25p for the second book, plus 15p per copy for each additional book ordered to a maximum charge of £1.90.

BFPO: 60p for the first book, 25p for the second book plus 15p per copy for the next 7 books, thereafter 9p per book

Overseas and Eire: £1.25 for the first book, 75p for the second book, thereafter 28p per book.

Credit card no: _____

Expiry Date: _____

Signature: _____

Lions reserve the right to show new retail prices on covers which may differ from those previously advertised in the text or elsewhere.

Some more titles in Lions Teen Tracks:

Some more titles in Lions Teen Tracks:

- ☐ **Slambash Wangs of a Compo Gormer**
  Robert Leeson £2.50
- ☐ **The Bumblebee Flies Anyway** *Robert Cormier* £1.95
- ☐ **After the First Death** *Robert Cormier* £2.25
- ☐ **That Was Then, This Is Now** *S E Hinton* £1.95
- ☐ **Centre Line** *Joyce Sweeney* £2.25

All these books are available at your local bookshop or newsagent, or to order direct from the publishers, just tick the titles you want and fill in the form below.

NAME (Block letters) _____

ADDRESS _____

_____

Send to: Collins Childrens Cash Sales, PO Box 11, Falmouth, Cornwall, TR10 9EP

I enclose a cheque or postal order or debit my Visa/Mastercard to the value of the cover price plus:

UK: 60p for the first book, 25p for the second book, plus 15p per copy for each additional book ordered to a maximum charge of £1.90.

BFPO: 60p for the first book, 25p for the second book plus 15p per copy for the next 7 books, thereafter 9p per book

Overseas and Eire: £1.25 for the first book, 75p for the second book, thereafter 28p per book.

Credit card no: _____

Expiry Date: _____

Signature: _____

Lions reserve the right to show new retail prices on covers which may differ from those previously advertised in the text or elsewhere.